We Exist in Each Other

Healing and Transforming in a Divisive World

Edith Alig Gagné
We Exist in Each Other

Book Design | Petya Tsankova
Editor | Kathie Lynas
Seva Publishing
Publishing Support | TSPA The Self Publishing Agency, Inc.

To all of us pursuing healing
and realization
of our True Selves

hello beautiful Self

In the midst of the darkest moments of the soul, it is my blessing that a spark ignites the pure light that you are and ripples out to all.

I bow to you

FOREWORD

First, let me just say that I *love* the title of this book: *We Exist in Each Other*. It speaks to the oneness, the universality, the interdependence, the coherence, collaboration, cooperation and collusion of all of Life and Its goodness and greatness that permeate everyone and everything in the cosmos. It speaks volumes of who and what we are, and why we are here on the planet.

Too often we think of ourselves as these entirely separate, lone entities going about life in our own bubbles with no connection to anyone or anything. There's even the saying, "We're born alone, and we'll die alone." Ideas like this fuel the erroneous belief that not only are we alone, but that feelings of loneliness and isolation – especially those borne of the painful effects of trauma and the accompanying feelings of powerlessness to change our lives – are normal and are a part of our identity. It also fuels larger false beliefs in division and separation amongst groups of people based on culture, family, "race" and other socially created and accepted markers of "difference" when, in Truth, each of us comes from a divine lineage that uniquely and infinitely expresses Itself in as many ways possible. To put it another way, instead of the idea of "out of many, one," it's time to embrace the Reality of "out of One, many."

Each of us are an aspect of a unified, whole existence, the powerful, creative God-presence, shot straight from the Eternal, here to expand Life and consciousness beyond what it has been, according to our distinctive patterns and expressions of talents and gifts. Experiences of pain and trauma, when understood within this broader context, can be the jumping-off point for discovering lessons we might not have otherwise learned, and from which beneficial new ideas get created that move us as a species, and our planet, forward beyond what we can presently imagine.

Through Edith's story, we get to witness what happens when we recognize and heed the invitation to acknowledge and realize our collective oneness with the omniscient, omnipotent, omnipresent Life Force that imbues and animates all living things. That even the deepest experiences of pain and trauma, feelings wholly caused by a belief that we are alone and separate from the innate love and goodness of the God-presence *that is us*, are absolutely no match for the power, intelligence and beauty we possess! I often say that instead of bringing your problem to God, show your problem how big your God is! When we accept this truism and move from shame, anger and resistance to the transcendent love and conscious connection with the divine that always awaits our acknowledgment, all perceived pain and problems dissolve in the mind of God.

This is what *We Exist in Each Other* demonstrates and celebrates.

Let Edith's journey show you the possibility that our life and very existence are not determined by the experience of trauma and pain. Allow it to inspire you towards healing and moving forward to live the life you are destined for, filled with the richness of joy, love and peace.

Michael Bernard Beckwith
Founder & CEO, Agape International Spiritual Center
Author, *Life Visioning and Spiritual Liberation*
& Host, *Take Back Your Mind* Podcast

ACKNOWLEDGEMENTS

The seeds for *We Exist In Each Other* were planted the moment I stood before my mother's body and first became aware of the words, "Your story needs to be told." Synchronicities before, during and after my mother's passing involving people, situations and events continued to show up. These experiences led to empowering messages of healing, transformation and joy, which manifested this book into fruition.

After years of not fully expressing or sharing my Truth, even though it flowed through me, my long-lingering desire to write a memoir exploded to the surface. After many years of nudges, messages and whispers, I finally said "yes" to writing this book!

At first, my curiosity led me to a podcast with host Anna Mullens interviewing Lori Bamber, which I later found out was called *How to use Storytelling to Heal: The True Story of Lori Bamber*. This instantly led me to Chief Operating Officer Ira Vergani at The Self Publishing Agency, Inc. (TSPA) and onto CEO and founder, Megan Williams. It was here when I actually made a commitment to do this work. I was led back to Anna Mullens, Chief Communications Officer (CCO) for TSPA, for an author branding session. Megan would connect me with the perfect editor and designer. Tage Lee, TSPA's Kindle Direct Publishing expert, provided support to make my book ready for electronic publishing. And Ira would set up a schedule to keep me moving forward. The TSPA team supported and guided me along the way to eventually publish this book. In this process I have found a whole new appreciation for authors and for the TSPA team.

A sincere thank you to Anna for using her voice to inspire other women, including me, to not only think about writing (and speaking) but to actually find my own authentic expression through the writing of this book.

An honourable thank you to Kathie Lynas, a senior editor at TSPA, whom I instantly knew was the perfect fit. Kathie supported the expression of my inner voice through my writing and helped bring my memoir out into the world in its purest form, as a book manuscript. I am forever grateful for your dedication and skill.

I am truly thankful to book cover and interior designer, Petya Tsankova, whose artistic flair and creative drive led to designs that perfectly synchronized with my vision. Petya definitely has a passion for creating beauty.

Special thanks to photographer Laura Paxton of Flashback Photo for capturing a state of calm inner peace.

I am deeply grateful to Rev. Dr. Michael Bernard Beckwith for saying "yes" when asked to write a foreword to my book. Michael is a New Thought minister, author, and founder and CEO of the Agape International Spiritual Center in Beverly Hills, California. He is one of the purest expressions of divinity in physical form that I've had the honour of crossing paths with. Thank you, Michael.

Thank you to the educators, health-care providers, friends, acquaintances and so-called strangers from all walks of life. Whether our lives intersect for just a moment or through an ongoing relationship, you have awakened me to what is not working and the ways in which we can be better. It is my hope that I awaken you, as well. A mirror of reflection of the pure light that we are, we rise in Truth.

Special thanks to non-profit organizations like Hospice North-west and the Elizabeth Fry Society of Northwestern Ontario, who have given me an opportunity to take sacred action to be of selfless service for the highest good of all. Your willingness and dedication to pave the way of making a difference in the lives of many of our most vulnerable individuals does not go unnoticed.

Also, a heartfelt thank you to informal caregivers who spend hours, days, months and years in compassionate love and care of a loved one. And to patients who surrender, putting all of their trust into the health-care team. I see and hear you. I feel you and treasure you within the boundless depths of my heart, for you have been called to this very important work of a higher calling.

To women who are incarcerated, many of whom have young innocent children, I feel your pain. In what can be a vicious cycle in an unjust, traumatized world, your light shines bright, offering an incredibly powerful message to the world. I believe in you.

Heartfelt gratitude to my precious children, Melissa, André and Corey, whose arrival into this world has shown me what a true miracle is. Your beauty, innocence and authenticity have taught me more than anything I could have possibly imagined. You have reminded me of the everlasting gift of the human spirit, our magnificence in connection to Mother Earth. To my son-in-law, Matej, my first grandchild, Mila, and my daughter-in-law, Stephanie, your love and commitment to this family is immeasurable.

Utmost appreciation to my loving husband, Pierre, who continues to inspire me in every given moment – I thank you. I have not only been blessed with you as the father of our children, you have given me space to be who I am in order to do this very important work. Your loyalty, commitment and caring is irreplaceable. I respect you for all that you are.

In honour of the fur babies in our growing family, who naturally connect us to our Higher Selves: Marty, our "grand-dog," and our "grand-cat," Pomme, both true Zen Masters.

To my siblings in Europe and Canada, your loving partners, and numerous nieces, and nephews – I feel you. May you return to inner peace through the divine presence of our human connection found within the very depths of our being.

Immense gratitude for my loving parents, Lorenz and Lieselotte, whose depth of intergenerational trauma rippling out through human suffering is the very spark that ignites my inner flame into action and strengthens me to live my unique purpose.

Thank you God, the Creator, for divine guidance through the act of sacred service for the betterment of all.

Finally, I thank you, the reader who picked up this book. It is through sharing our stories that we connect to the higher consciousness that is us. I admire your willingness to explore this unique expression of the oneness that we are by looking deeper into this book. To you, I remain forever in Truth.

"Nothing real can be threatened.
Nothing unreal exists."

A Course in Miracles

MESSAGE
TO MY READERS

Dear friends,

I felt inspired to share the story of my life's journey, the path I have taken that led me to where I am today – connecting with people from around the world through my contribution to help heal collective trauma.

Each of us has our own path to follow, and I know that my experiences won't apply to everyone. But I hope that I can bring you something that you will find valuable. My goal is to share how I have been affected by family and individual trauma, how I have moved through and past its effects, and how I have found ways to tap into an inner intelligence that breaks me out of our fabricated human story and guides me to connect with others in empathy and compassion.

Have you ever known something for certain even though there was no "real-world evidence" to support it? Have you ever received inexplicable "signals" deep within yourself that told you something was definitely going to happen or that directed you to take specific action? I have had many moments in my life like this, where I have sensed a connection to a higher intelligence, a divine wisdom.

For a long time, I kept it all to myself. At times feeling alone in this divisive world, I knew through a deeper intelligence that I am never alone. That knowledge comes from within, not without. That this inner knowing is available to everyone. And from here, we are all spiritual leaders.

In order to fit into this fast-paced world of uncertainty, which leaves many people anxious and exhausted, I sought to connect with like-hearted people pursuing higher levels of consciousness. In this human connection is an opportunity to support our growth. I hope my story will show you that although you may feel alone, you are actually never alone.

If we connect to each other, we can have so much more impact for others in our lives and for humanity as a whole. As each of us struggles to overcome the darkness in the world and free ourselves from the domain of the ego and the thoughts that divide us, we can contribute to a bigger effort to heal humanity.

Like all human beings, I was born into a divisive world and had parents who carried with them the wounds and scars of past generations and the events of their own lives.

Both my parents lived through the trauma of war. My mother in particular responded to this suffering by burying it, by avoiding the painful conversations. Mother relied on toxic silence as a protective shield against the suffering, and her undigested layers of trauma were passed on to me.

As a child, I was a witness to a devastating disease crisis affecting my father. Again, my mother's instinctive response was to remain silent. She lovingly supported my father through his ill health for many years, but as a family we didn't discuss or confront the suffering. So, I didn't have the opportunity to process it and it remained as my own frozen trauma, with impacts that would show up later in my life.

Yet the disease crisis I witnessed also opened up a connection in me. In the moment, I was able to separate myself from my fearful thoughts and to tap into a state of calm presence, where

I was at peace with what was happening – no expectation, no judgement. It was a gateway to a deeper silence – the healing power of silence in presence with Spirit.

The portal had opened, and through my life, I have found ways to connect with this inner resource. It has guided me to take conscious healing action in the world and to be of service, first as an informal caregiver to my father, then on to palliative care, and as a facilitator of meditation for incarcerated women. And in my most recent mission, to explore the healing of trauma within the collective.

In a world going through so much darkness right now, a world of division which keeps on repeating itself, we can find the hope to come out of it. By going within, we can access the magical spark that connects us in empathy, compassion and love.

Part One:
THE CALL TO HEAL TRAUMA

"In war, truth is the first casualty."

Aeschylus

"Nothing in all creation is so like God as silence."

Meister Eckhart

"War is like night, she said. It covers everything."

Elie Weisel

I felt an internal push to visit Szczecin, Poland, formerly Stettin in Germany, where my mother and many family members were either displaced or killed during World War II. I wanted to get in touch with my mother's story – to experience the city that was once part of her happy youth and then the source of unimaginable pain and loss.

I needed to connect with the trees, grass and flowers, with the sun shining on rivers and the formation of clouds in the skies. I wanted to wear a dress and have a glass of champagne to celebrate the moments I saw in the black-and-white pre-war photographs Mother had shared with me. Those photos captured my teenaged mother and her friends gathered outdoors with smiles on their faces. Oh, how I would love to be able to listen to them laugh as they engaged in conversation way back in 1936.

I wanted to find anything left that had outlived the bombings of this beautiful city once part of Germany, now belonging to Poland.

For the most part, my mother didn't want to confront the wounds of war in her life. As a child, I witnessed her silence and felt her pain.

As I was drawn to visit my mother's home, I was also being called to shatter the silence about the horrors and to break the cycle of intergenerational trauma – to speak on behalf of my mother. It was a calling I could no longer put on the shelf to deal with later. I believed it was my responsibility to be seen, to be heard and to connect with others on a global level. I wanted to do my part to help humanity process the layers of trauma. This calling was so much bigger than me.

All my life, I had been deepening my spiritual knowledge to overcome the culturally imposed limitations of a divisive world. I had cultivated my connection with divine intelligence and the ability to observe what was happening in the world with a calm state of presence. And I had a practice of service to others. Now, I had a new mission.

I was led to a worldwide community, a "sangha" as it is known in Buddhism, people coming together in collective meditation, movement and presence. Timeless Wisdom Training (TWT) is a program offered by the Academy of Inner Science, founded by Thomas Hübl, a spiritual teacher and author, including of the book *Healing Collective Trauma: A Process for Integrating Our Intergenerational and Cultural Wounds.*

I was drawn to the description of the program on its website: "Timeless Wisdom Training is a community of committed practitioners coming together over a two-year period to support one another, to work on personal, group and ancestral trauma, and to learn conscious growth tools, practices and methods." It was offered online, and we would meet in person not too far from my mother's birthplace in Germany. Even closer was Bremerhaven, a one-hour drive from the port she left to emigrate to Canada. In October of 1955, Mother left on the ship called the *Arosa Star*, for the journey from Germany to Quebec City, Canada.

I would join in connection with fellow human beings from all walks of life, coming from various countries, languages and cultures. Together, we would engage in somatic awareness practices, advanced meditation practices and transformational processes that would address individual and collective undigested trauma passed on through many generations. This was a divine opportunity to come together for healing, globally.

It was what I was longing for. Within individual, collective and intergenerational trauma, there is a gift, gems to be uncovered to guide humanity through our suffering.

SEPARATION THROUGH THE TRAUMA OF WAR

When I first learned of this story about one of my ancestors, it gave me hope that connection is possible even during a divisive war.

He was named Julian-Nicolas Rèche, known as "Arnould," and was born in France in 1838. During the Franco-Prussian War of 1870, less than 50 years before World War I ended, he cared for the medical and spiritual needs of the wounded French and German soldiers who fought in the trenches. Blessed Brother Arnold Rèche died at the age of 52 and was beatified by Pope John Paul II in 1987. His grave became known as a site for miraculous healings.

Of course, connection and healing are only part of the story of war. My heart aches for the suffering and loss my parents went through during wartime, earlier in their lives.

World War I had just begun when my father, Lorenz, was born as the youngest son in a large family. His mother was French-born and his father was born in Switzerland. In 1917, when Father was just three years old, he experienced his first traumatic loss, his family torn apart and his country lost.

During WWI, the German Empire occupied parts of northeast France, and in the course of that occupation, the German army separated my father's family. As the story has been passed on, my Papi (grandfather) and Mamie (grandmother) were forced to leave their home in Tarquimpol with the younger half of their children, including my three-year-old father. While the older children were left behind in France, my grandparents took the youngest children to Switzerland, a country that remained neutral during World War I, as it did in World War II.

Father lived most of his young life in the Canton of Graubünden in the Swiss Alps. He shared with me and my siblings some of his memories of that time. In this mountainous alpine area, where he often skied, Father spoke of the Edelweiss plant known to be a national symbol in Switzerland. This mountain flower symbolizes deep love and devotion. It is said the plant grows high in the mountains above the tree line and is forbidden to be picked. Years later, father emigrated to Canada to be with his two older brothers, who had emigrated earlier.

My mother, Lieselotte, was from Stettin, Germany, located near the Baltic Sea. During World War II, Allied air raids in 1944 and heavy fighting between the German and Soviet armies destroyed 65 per cent of Stettin's buildings and almost all of the city centre, the seaport and local industries. The Soviet Red Army captured the city on April 26, 1945. It was during this time, just before the end of World War II in Europe, when Oma, my grandmother, may have been killed.

It was difficult to learn the truth because my mother didn't ever tell me about her mother's death. Throughout the years, I heard different stories, shared in whispers. One of my mother's friends passed on one version that she said Mother had privately shared with her.

This friend said that during heavy bombing, my mother and her parents were hiding in the cellar of their home, when my grandmother suddenly ran upstairs to save a hope chest for her daughters. She never returned. Another source said Oma was killed when a bomb hit the house. Yet another person said the Soviets entered the home and cut my grandmother's beautiful long hair before murdering her. God only knows what occurred during this horrific experience that numbed and silenced my mother. It's possible that my mother was pregnant during this time (although I was never able to confirm when Oma was murdered), a reminder that birth and even the natural death of loved ones continue during the horrors of war.

Internally displaced, amid fear during wartime, my mother and grandfather had survived World War II, but at a terrible cost. They carried within them the deep-rooted layers of traumatic memories of horrific visions, sounds and smells, the effects of ancestral trauma, shame and survivors' guilt over the unimaginable and the loss of a wife and mother. Within a few months, the city they had at one time called home no longer existed as Stettin, Germany. In October of that year, it became a part of Poland and was restored to its historic Polish name, Szczecin.

Mother was not only separated from her mother, the grand-mother of her soon-to-be-born infant, but the entire family, including aunts, uncles, nieces, nephews and others who were either killed or displaced. Separation from friends, neighbours and a familiar life, not knowing who had survived or who had been murdered. Businesses and homes they worked so hard for, now demolished, many burned to ash.

A number of years passed before Lieselotte emigrated to Canada, where my parents met one another for the first time. Each one separated from their families through war, they came together and created a family in a new country called Canada.

FORGET WAR

I have a vivid memory of when I first began to understand my mother's trauma from her war experiences. It was the month of April, and the television was on and broadcasting a documentary about World War II. The anniversary of the end of the war in Europe was approaching – the surrender of the German armed forces to the Allies on May 7, 1945.

Horrific black and white images of battle flickered on the television. I stood there watching when my mother entered the living room with a look of fury on her face and abruptly shut off the TV, saying, "*Warum können sie es nicht einfach vergessen?*" My parents routinely spoke German in the home. She was saying, "Why can't they just forget about it?"

As I write these words, I am brought to tears. So many years later, I can still feel my mother's deep-rooted inner pain. It's a part of me. "Forget war" because it could stir up the undigested layers of trauma frozen in time – a wound so deep there were no words to describe the darkness. No words were available, so Mother rarely, if ever, spoke to me of WWII.

Father would often watch war documentaries on his own, but he protected my mother from being exposed to them. He had once said, "*Mama hat so viel durchgemacht mit dem Krieg,*" which meant, "Mama went through so much during the war." "She went through hell." Now as an adult, I think about this "hell on earth" that she endured, along with so many others. Suffering created by the thoughts, words and actions of those before us, passed on through the generations, stuck in a repetitive play of ego, still played out to this day.

Mother was the kindest, most loving and compassionate woman, and I ached to see her hurting so deeply and retreating into silence. Who was I or anyone to judge her for refusing to speak the unspeakable?

After all, she had experienced war as a German citizen during the Third Reich in Stettin, the home she ultimately had to flee.

As I learned more about the effects of trauma, I came to understand that seeing those images could have easily triggered shame, guilt or post-traumatic stress disorder (PTSD) in Mother. I also remember her sometimes exhibiting fear when there was a knock on the door of our home during the evening hours. I recall her looking startled and freezing in place, if only for a moment.

After I had seen my mother's discomfort over the war documentary, I connected with her experience myself, when we studied the Second World War in history class. At first I didn't pay too much attention to what was being taught, knowing it pained so many people, like my mother. Not all students in my class, if any, had a German-born parent who had lived under the regime of Nazi Germany. Part of me internalized my mother's self-protection; I thought why focus on the past when it's already done?

Did the teacher even know Mother lived in Germany during World War II? Was he aware of her pain and suffering, ancestral pain and suffering, which, although invisible, was also a part of me, his student? I thought, surely he must know. After all, we lived in a small community where my mother worked in public and had a strong German accent.

Black and white photos in the history books spoke for themselves. I learned what the Nazi Party run by Adolf Hitler had done to the Jewish people and other innocent human beings: they were taken away from their homes, held in concentration camps and so many were murdered. Six million Jews were exterminated just because they were Jewish! The more I learned, the more horrified I became.

And what about all the innocent German civilians now traumatized at the end of war who had become targets just to prove a point. Surely not all were guilty. When World War II allies went after Germany, many civilian centres surrounding the military targets were also bombed, on purpose, to make sure the Germans would know they were defeated. My mother, my beautiful pregnant mother, was a German civilian caught up in the hideous actions that came out of mad minds, a projection of collective insanity. Surely, my mother shouldn't have to be stained by the very fact of being German at this time in history.

I could feel myself sink deeper and deeper within. This was really touching close to home. Conflicted, I was becoming more and more tense, and I began to constrict myself even further, building an invisible barrier around me. I wanted to run and hide.

Holding my breath, I couldn't speak in class, swallowing and suppressing the feelings wanting to come to the surface, adding another layer of trauma because I had no safe space for expression or to exhale. My mother wished the world could forget war, and I couldn't utter a single word to contribute to the topic of war at school. An invisible, unspeakable effect of trauma was passed on from mother to child. The silent suffering not only included my mother; it included me too.

One day when I returned home from high school, mother shared a couple of black-and-white photos taken a few years before the beginning of the war. In each photo, she was a teenager (although a bit older), just like me. One of the photos was from her shoulders up. I observed everything about her in detail. In this photo frozen in time, I looked at her hairstyle, eyebrows, eyes, nose, mouth, teeth, jewellery and clothing. Mother was so beautiful to look at and she looked so happy. I noticed that on the photograph, a small area on part of her blouse had been scribbled over with a pen.

In another photo, mother was sitting with young men and women at a table, happily in conversation over food and drink. Again, on this picture, a pen had been used to obscure part of her shirt. I later learned beneath this scribble was the swastika symbol used during a time when Adolf Hitler was the Chancellor of Germany and head of the totalitarian regime known as the Third Reich. Mother was born into the era of the Nazi Party that created and supported the ideology of Nazism. Many Germans were groomed at a young age in groups like "Young Girls' League" and "Faith and Beauty Society." In 1936, juveniles were forced to be a member of "Hitler Youth" or "League of German Girls in Hitler Youth." An innocent teenager, did Mother work for the government before the Second World War began in 1939? Was she the one who had hidden the swastika in shame? She never explained and I never asked.

WE MUST REMEMBER

In school, I learned of a Canadian poet and physician by the name of Lieutenant-Colonel John McCrae, who in 1915 had written the famous war poem "In Flanders Fields." We were drawing poppies in class, when I felt a beautiful connection to Mother Earth and started thinking about a human battle in the midst of nature.

I wondered, "Why couldn't everyone just get along?"

I imagined soldiers running through battlefields amongst wild-flowers including vibrant red and black-coloured poppies – the beauty of nature representing the Light, while these young men were fighting in the darkness of a mind-created war. I learned poppies grew on the battlefields after World War I ended and continue to be used today as a symbol of both remembrance and hope for a peaceful future.

"Lest We Forget" is a phrase commonly used in war remem-brance services. As I thought about this phrase and about the power of the poppy as a symbol, my mind expanded. I better un-derstood my mother's desire to forget war, common to so many. I thought about the soldiers who never spoke of war when they returned home, perhaps as a way to protect others and them-selves from further trauma, feeling they had to suffer in silence. At the same time, I knew deep in my heart that we must never forget war and that we must speak about it. Deep within I knew there is light, a gift, the Real Truth of who we are, in this hor-rific darkness.

We should never forget the sacrifices that women, men and chil-dren make during war. We are them. They are us.

I felt discussions of war validated some of what had happened in the past, and it was so important for humanity to not only learn from the mistakes, in order to not repeat them, but to dig deep into our own trauma to discover sacred gifts waiting to be discovered and to be used in our lives today.

These moments when I was younger helped lead me on the path to processing historical trauma in a global community.

I write these words for my mother, who found it too painful to speak of war, and for my Oma, who never had the chance to speak. In silence, I am called to be the voice of the voiceless.

Part Two:
OPENING THE DOOR TO DIVINE INTELLIGENCE

"From the moment of your birth a ladder was placed before you to help you escape."

Jalal ad-Din Muhammad Rumi

"The miracle of life is ageless, born in time but nourished in eternity."

A Course in Miracles

I remember connecting with what I now call "higher intelligence" or "mysticism" at a young age, which is common for many of us as children. In our earlier years, we remain closer to our divine origins, but over time, the divisions of the human experience take over and we "forget" that easy connection to infinite wisdom.

During my childhood, my most powerful spiritual experiences arose from immersion in nature, supported by the fact that our family lived in a number of remote and smaller communities that existed within rich natural environments. I remember the wonder I felt in the presence of animals and flowers and the pure joy of feeling the sun and the wind.

Our journey in human form sees us conditioned into the world of opposites. Our task is to "escape," as Rumi describes it – to step back from the divisions and our unproductive thinking patterns and restore our links to that greater wisdom.

During a serious health crisis with my father, I found myself suddenly connecting with this higher intelligence. The event was shocking and it would have been natural for me to be upset and fearful. But at that moment, in part because of my mother's gentle presence, I found myself calm and accepting of the reality before me.

A portal to divine intelligence was opened for me at that moment, and throughout my life, I continued my efforts to strengthen these bonds.

I have learned that being open and having the courage to allow absolute, infinite intelligence to come through us takes our lives to a level where we can heal together.

Accepting and embracing this divine guidance is available to each one of us and helps us discover our unique purpose in the world.

I AM ALIVE

A timeless, formless, ageless being, I arrive in a separate human form. As a newborn, I lay listless with a bump protruding from the top of my head. My European parents, relatively new to this country of Canada, feared I could die.

Mother felt a desperate need to write a letter to a dear friend, who was 7,000 kilometres away, to seek advice on how to save her infant. Finally, the letter arrived from her friend, delivered through the mail to the secluded northern Ontario community where we lived.

Here was the advice: Mother was to purchase a pear, which is known to symbolize immortality, inner peace and eternal life. She was instructed to cut the pear in half and cut out the core, which included seeds and the seed-bearing ovary wall. Mother proceeded to gently rub each half of the fruit over the bump on the top of my head, while repeating an affirmative prayer. In the following days, the wound on the top of my head began to vanish, bringing immense joy to the hearts of my parents and hope for a new life coming into the world. The beginning of my life's journey in this impermanent human form would continue.

My first encounter with a possible death was at birth. But the essential life force, giving life to all living beings, prevailed and flowed like a river throughout my physical body. Born of Love, I am fully alive as I dance the cosmic rhythm of Life. I am nowhere and everywhere. Timeless in a world of time, unchanged in a world where change is constant.

I arrive as a temporary guest with an assignment, a unique purpose. It would take me time and experience to discover what it was.

I was born in the small community of Umfreville, in the Kenora District of the province of Ontario, Canada. In recognition of the Indigenous peoples who were the early guardians of the land here, it is also known as the traditional territory of the Anishinaabe Nation of Treaty #3. To those of us living in this remote, Northern Ontario community, it was simply "the bush." At the time of my birth, people living in Umfreville were a mix of cultures, speaking such languages as Ojibway, French, German and English.

My parents called me Edith, a name that came from the Old English word "Eadgyo" – a combination of "ead," meaning "riches" or "blessed," and "gyo," meaning "war." The full name meant "prosperous in strife."

My identification through form identity had begun and would develop further, according to the beliefs of my parents and society.

The Umfreville area is located along Highway 642 southeast of Sioux Lookout and is named after Edward Umfreville, a fur trader who passed through, back in 1784. Wildlife, especially black bears, frequented the Umfreville area, and every now and again, they were lured by the scent of garbage, along with meals prepared in a nearby bush camp for a company my father worked for.

Our house was nestled in the middle of the bush surrounded by rough terrain, close to the train tracks and a few steps from the lake where a bush plane often landed.

Transportation to and from this wooded area was by rail, vehicle or float plane. In an emergency situation, the hand car (a small car powered by people) was used on the railway tracks as a form of passenger service. As a matter of fact, it was one way my then-pregnant mother was transported more than 50 kilometres from our home to the nearest hospital to give birth to one of my older siblings.

My playground was, and still is, the bush. For the first three years of life, exploring the land gave me an early connection to spiritual intelligence – a link to something greater than me and a sense of belonging. Although I didn't have the same words to describe it as a child, I remember the feelings that came from connecting to the natural world.

The elements of air that I breathe, the breath that breathes me, the healing water of the river of my soul flowing within and without. I am grounded in the very earth I crawl and walk on, the space within and between, interwoven within the fabric of my being. My sense of taste, touch, smell, sight and sound are fully alive. Nature is here; nature is everywhere. I am Earth. I am Life.

STRAIGHT OUT OF THE BUSH

A few years passed and now, as a healthy three-year old toddler, I joined my parents and older siblings in moving out of the bush to continue the journey that would one day awaken me to my purpose. I was the same age my father had been when he began his perilous journey away from his first home in France.

We first headed southeast to a place called Ignace, Ontario. I have one particularly vivid memory from this time, when I first heard the newborn cries of my youngest sibling, born at home. I remember Mother standing up holding her infant, both of them naked, and with a smile on her face, then introducing me to my baby sibling. Later that day, Father arrived home from work and my older siblings returned from school to find Mother, now fully dressed, holding a bundled-up new family member. Our Canadian family was growing.

A few years later, we continued on our path, relocating to another small Ontario community called Wabigoon. The name "Wabigoon" comes from the Ojibwe word waabogon, meaning "marigold," or wasabi-miigwan, "white feather." It was here on Wabigoon Lake where my father and I went fishing, and I caught my very first fish.

FREEDOM – CHILDREN LIVING IN HARMONY WITH NATURE

The Trans-Canada Highway runs through the entire country of Canada from the Atlantic Coast to the Pacific Coast, including right through the community of Wabigoon. Although we didn't live as deep in the bush as we once did, Wabigoon is built amidst nature, and I was in constant awe of the gifts offered by the natural world.

Painted turtles are common in northwestern Ontario. Every time I found one, I'd pick it up and admire the amazing, colourful markings. Whenever I held a turtle in my hands I could feel the strength of this slow-moving reptile. I felt the energy of its four webbed feet powerfully move in an effort to escape the grips of my hands. I was in awe of the patterns and hues I found when I turned it over to explore its underside, which I later learned is called the plastron.

Did you know that counting the rings on the scutes (the bony plate) on the shell of a painted turtle is similar to counting the dark rings on the stump of a tree? For both turtle and tree, counting the rings tells you its age. I was fascinated, to say the least. While turning the turtle over, I explored the colourful underside and in a state of presence, with the painted turtle in my hands, I remained engaged and mesmerized.

One day while walking in the bush, I saw the most beautiful flower I had ever seen. It reminded me of a slipper, and I was thrilled when I found out it was actually called a pink lady's slipper, known in Ojibwe as ma-ki-sin-waa-big-waan, a "moccasin flower." An adult advised me to never pick this flower – the pink lady's slipper takes up to 10 years to flower.

It reminded me of the wild Edelweiss in the high altitudes of Switzerland, the flower of my father's childhood. It too was not to be picked. These were powerful messages about the need to protect nature's masterpieces.

Nature connected me to divine intelligence, but like all humans, I sometimes lost that connection. I have a vivid memory of the first time I became aware of my egoic mind – the thoughts and judgements that separate us from other people and from pure consciousness and the wisdom it brings.

It was when we were living in Wabigoon, and I was five years old. I had joined a group of children, some older, some younger, who were playing on a dirt road named Bay Street, at the bottom of a very large hill. It seemed that everyone had quickly paired up with friends of a similar age – everyone but me, that is.

Not getting enough attention from the others, I imagined myself riding bareback on a huge black stallion. In my mind's eye, I was sitting up high, much higher than the huge hill, much higher than the children below me, almost flying up towards the sky. I thought, "Maybe now they will see me and want to play with me too."

The mind's constrictions and labels that divide us can often cut us off from the expansiveness of the heart's connection to all.

As I grew older and made it to high school, I would find myself dominated more by my thinking mind. The divine connection I had forged through nature was always there but seemed to feel distant at times. Without a natural expression of this intelligence, I would begin to question where I fit in, and I fell into the ways of the ego of separation while trying to figure it out.

A SHIFT IN ENERGY

Together, my parents provided a safe space of connection, trust, acceptance and nourishment for our family. Mother was a hands-on primary caregiver, a loving presence. I admired her external and internal beauty from afar.

For a long time, my father was the main breadwinner, responsible for financially providing for the family. His job was a "bush worker," someone who worked on the land, he told us.

Father enjoyed working, and he often had a smile on his face when returning home. I remember those days when his happiness was steady and reassuring; all was right with my world.

But I began to notice something was changing in him. His smiles were less frequent, and I would often hear him moan in pain. I continued to play in silence with an increased alertness to those sounds and other signs that he wasn't well. These moments would increase and decline, only to increase and decline again.

I have a strong memory of the string of white pearls Mother wore around her neck. One day, when I was in Grade 1, I asked her if I could borrow her pearls to wear to school for picture day. Mother agreed, as long as I kept them around my neck until I returned home, which I did. It felt as if I had brought a piece of Mommy to school with me that day. I was so happy to share this special moment with her. During this time, I seemed to want a stronger human connection with Mother, perhaps because Father was becoming ill.

Eventually, Father's ill health would lead to loss, with precious moments no longer possible to share. Earlier, on the days when he felt well, Father would take me or one of my siblings for a ride with him to the restaurant at the Central Hotel in Dryden, a town about 20 kilometres away. This was a special time that I looked forward to; it was our one-on-one quality time.

I remember those drives in our family vehicle, a Chevrolet car in the colour officially called "Roman Red." Once we arrived, we'd each order our favourite pie – apple for both Father and me – another cherished connection.

Our father-daughter quality time became less frequent until the point where our rides to Dryden halted altogether. As Father's health continued to decline, our familiar family life eroded further. My father could no longer drive, and since my mother didn't drive, we would have to sell the family vehicle. My parents decided we needed to move to Dryden, a larger community with resources to support our increased needs.

In Dryden, my parents' traditional roles quickly reversed. Because Father could no longer work, he remained in the home, and Mother entered the working world as a saleswoman in a clothing store. This disruption in traditional gender roles taught me that it was okay for either the man or woman, or both, to provide for the family or to stay at home, to cook and clean.

It was wonderful to see that Mother had a more intense inner glow when she returned to the workplace. She loved to dress up and told us that she had fond memories of working as a salesgirl when she was a young woman in Germany.

EDUCATION – FEAR-BASED THINKING CREEPING IN

I was joyful, excited and content with whatever occurred in this new town. On many hot summer days, we would walk to a nearby restaurant, count the change one of our parents had given us, and then lay it on the counter to purchase an ice cream cone. A special summer treat no child could resist.

During the summertime in Dryden, I joyfully played along with my siblings and a couple of other children we met in our new neighbourhood. We would skip, play hopscotch and ride our bikes through mud puddles, and when no one was looking, we stole crab apples from a neighbour's tree. But my most powerful experiences came from engagement with nature.

The boys and I searched for garter snakes, picking them up from under rocks out on a cliff near the highway. Another joyful pursuit was catching tadpoles and putting them in a container of pond water so we could observe them before setting them free to remain healthy and to eventually evolve into frogs.

I remember one particularly intense interaction with the natural environment, shortly after we first moved to Dryden.

One evening, not long after settling into our new home, I looked out into the dark night through the window of my bedroom. My eyes wide open, I saw a black bear staring back at me before it turned around and walked away. I stood still in a moment of silence before I immediately ran to my family to tell them what I had just seen. But when we returned to the bedroom window, there was no bear in sight.

When we had lived in the bush up north, I had heard the adults saying it was not unheard of for a bear to put its paws up to a window and take a peek inside. Did I actually see a bear through my window? Did it run away after I saw it? Was it a true childhood memory or was it imagination?

Still, I knew there was a bear out there somewhere. Getting ready to go to bed for the night, before closing my eyes, I said goodnight to the black bear. In this knowing, I felt an inner peace, a divine connection to Mother Earth and her creatures. Overall, it was a magical moment, and although we now lived among many more people in our new community, my connection to wildlife remained strong.

I would soon attend Grade 2 in a new school, and for the most part, I was excited to meet and play with all of the children.

But beneath the surface, there were brief moments when I felt a fearful feeling creeping up within. It was the same kind of feeling I had felt in my earlier years, right before I had imagined myself on a flying black stallion. Feeling fearful of the future is a perfect example of how the mind can deceive us and fuel our anxiety.

The day was finally here. Once I arrived at school, I didn't know anyone my age, and many of the other students appeared to know one another. And although I still felt excited, I kept imagining the other children rejecting me, not wanting to play with me.

It all got to be too much one morning. While walking to school, I crossed a set of train tracks before I quickly turned around with tears running down my eyes to return home as fast as my feet would take me. I couldn't help but silently think repetitive thoughts, "Will they want to play with me too? I'm so scared."

When I arrived home, I had a discussion with Father about the fear of going to this new school, which included more children than I had ever seen. Father knew how important it was to create a safe space for me, to allow me to feel my feelings without shame and to express my tangled thoughts. This was one of the times in my life when I felt the power of truly listening to someone else without judgement, feeling how we can connect with another person when being together in silence. The power of sacred silence and deep listening.

Father gently listened while I shared, and eventually, he took me by the hand. Together, we walked a couple of blocks before he nudged me to walk on my own the rest of the way. When I arrived at the entrance of the new school, I already felt better.

As time went on, I became more comfortable with the school and made many new friends. This environment was giving me a lot of joy.

Every morning, our day began with the Lord's Prayer, followed by the singing of the national anthem, O Canada. We were led in prayer and song by a voice that came out of the PA system, heard by everyone in every classroom or office. Whether or not we could see one another inside the school, students and staff stood up together. It was at this very moment when barriers dissolved. Regardless of the grade we were in, our age, skin colour and life situation, we were connected in silence through presence.

It was so peaceful. I felt a deep sense of belonging in the school environment like never before. An invisible space opened, a doorway, a portal to go deeper within. And whether we were aware of it or not, we connected in Oneness.

At other times of the day, anxious thoughts would still intrude –
worries about whether my friends would include me continued
to arise but also new fears about Father – was he all right back
at home and why did he have so much pain?

The clouded thoughts would generate feelings of sadness along
with physical sensations in my body, tension and discomfort. I
never spoke to anyone about these fear-based thoughts and un-
pleasant emotions. This was the unhealthy form of silence, the
suppression of difficult emotions. They became an undigested
layer within me, trauma at the personal level. And hiding my
truth more frequently separated me from others as I observed
the world.

Still, saying the Lord's Prayer and singing O Canada together
at the beginning of a school day calmed my thinking mind and
centred me. I felt at ease in connection through presence, if only
for a moment.

CONSCIOUS AWARENESS

At home, I became increasingly aware of subtle changes continuing to happen within our family. The energy around Father seemed to be getting ever heavier. He was still not feeling well, and in fact, it seemed he was getting worse and was now experiencing stronger internal pain.

During each moan from my father, I was also aware of Mother's alert presence, an invisible connection within all of us. In a calm state, she assisted Father in any way imaginable, and at the same time, comforted the children. She was a natural caregiver, and my eyes were glued to her every move.

And then it happened. A health crisis burst into our world.

It was in the middle of the night. I was asleep in my bedroom and was suddenly awakened by voices. I jumped out of bed and quietly walked towards the sounds; the painful moans of Father were familiar, but this time, they were louder, more frequent, a different tone. I saw Father standing over the toilet bowl in the nearby washroom with Mother by his side. His face was pale and drawn, when a gush of blood shot out of his mouth into the bowl.

I was 10 years old, and I couldn't look away.

I noticed a large empty ice cream pail from a nearby restaurant had somehow found its way into our home and was quickly used as a bucket for the blood. Father then sat on the lid of the toilet bowl and between pauses where he tried to catch his breath, he spit blood into the pail. I managed to get a glimpse when I peeked into the old ice cream pail and saw a lot of blood mixed with bathroom tissue.

I stood still. I remained alert in a state of deep timeless presence. As an alert witness in a depth of profound inner stillness, I remained calm.

I slowly made my way to the steps of the staircase. I peeked between the railings, as I continued to watch Mother support Father. She was also alert, the calm in the midst of a disease crisis. In an effort to protect the children, in a soft voice, Mother said, "Go back into your bedroom." In an attempt to partially follow my mother's directions, I moved over a few more steps before finding a hiding spot and continued to peek between the railing running along the top of the steps. I had a good view of Father in the washroom. I was attentive to every move.

I remained an ever-present witness as I watched more blood pour out of Father's mouth in repeated bursts. He appeared to become weaker and weaker, and his face turned a deathly pale, as every bit of energy was sucked out of him. Mother continued to calmly assist him, and I too remained calm.

SILENCE OVER WORDS

I felt a shift in consciousness: in expanded awareness, I observed it all. The physical form of Father during pain and suffering, the form of Mother, a survivor of war, and my own physical self as a witness. Effortless grace in action. I had no thoughts, no words, only silence.

There is something so profound in stillness, in silence, in the face of a disease crisis. "The silence is so loud." That was my impression of the experience and it was a theme that would play out throughout my life. This was the powerful, affirming form of silence, the place where we can rise above human suffering and connect with a greater, healing intelligence. I had become mute in the face of what I observed and built a safe container around myself that allowed me to be an observer, a watcher of life at play.

In the spaciousness of my mother's calm presence, I connected to the depth of profound inner peace. I wasn't entangled in the pain and suffering happening before me. I didn't know it in an intellectual way, nor did I have the language to express it. In a dimension beyond the mind, meditation led.

I would later find out that immutable presence in the midst of the wound would be the very foundation of my assignment, my unique purpose in this world. I knew there was hope in all of this suffering.

This was the portal to higher intelligence, a calm acceptance of what exists. No rebellion against what is.

∞

The ambulance arrived outside our home to take Father to the emergency department. Two paramedics quickly walked through the door holding a stretcher and strapped him onto it. I was glad his body was on the thin side, so he would fit on the stretcher and at least have some comfort. They carried him down the steep narrow staircase, and before the front door closed behind them, I heard him whisper in a weak voice, "Pray for me."

I ran to my parents' bedroom window where I could get a better view of Father as the paramedics loaded him into the ambulance before closing the doors and driving off. Still imbued with silence, I remained at the window staring blankly into the dark night.

Not far from my parents' bedroom was the doorway to the basement, where Father frequently worked at repairing different appliances – not only for us but also for people in the neighbourhood. Being able to do something to help others gave him a sense of purpose. During happy moments, I would hear him whistling in the basement while he kept himself busy.

He particularly enjoyed working on meticulous items like the inner workings of a clock. We had a couple around the house, and he would often take them apart in small pieces before putting them back together to make sure they all rang at the exact same time. An incredible amount of patience was needed. Perhaps this fascination with clocks had something to do with our Swiss roots.

I walked towards the opened door to the basement, and as I looked down into the darkness at the bottom of the stairs, I heard a whispered, pain-filled call: "Help me." I went to Mother and said, "I just heard Father downstairs calling for help."

Perhaps the opening of the portal made this connection with my father possible.

She assured me that couldn't be the case. My father was in the ambulance on his way to the hospital to see the doctor who would help him. We didn't speak about what had just happened. Each one of us needed a moment in spaciousness to be with what we had just witnessed.

I returned to my bedroom upstairs and got into my bed, when I remembered Father had asked us to pray for him. A couple of tears rolled down my cheeks, as I lay on my pillow silently repeating the only prayer I knew, the Lord's Prayer, which I had learned at school.

Our Father,
Who art in heaven
hallowed be Thy Name.
Thy Kingdom come.
Thy will be done on earth,
as it is in heaven.
Give us this day our daily bread.
And forgive us for our trespasses,
as we forgive those who
trespass against us.
And lead us not into temptation,
but deliver us from evil.
For Thine is the Kingdom,
the power, and the glory,
forever and ever.
Amen

SUPPRESSION OF THE TRAUMA

Before long, morning arrived, and everyone, my mother, my siblings and I silently did our part without complaint or resistance. Regardless of what we had witnessed in darkness, life as we knew it continued, and now it was time to go to school.

Once there, I went through the motions of following my normal school routine. I observed the teacher teaching the class, played with my friends outside during recess and ate lunch.

Everyone around me was oblivious to what I had witnessed. There were moments at school when my ego would plant dark thoughts in my mind – thoughts that replayed the past making me sad and thoughts about the future making me afraid: "Will Father come back? Is he going to die?"

In the coming days, I bounced between the peaceful calm presence I had felt when watching my father bleeding, and the thoughts generated by my mind, which played out the worst possible scenarios. I bounced from mind to heart, heart to mind. There were deep moments when the heart and mind connected where I was at peace in this emptiness.

But there was also another form of silence that was more destructive. My family and I didn't speak about the disturbing scenes we had witnessed the previous night. I didn't have an opportunity to fully process my experience and feelings in a safe space. I didn't know how to digest and integrate it into my young life. Instead, not knowing how or what to say, I would swallow the very undigested twords and feelings that needed to be expressed.

I remained silent and the seeds of suppressed trauma were planted. I had also inherited unconscious emotional legacies from my parents and grandparents who had been traumatized themselves from war.

I would feel the impacts of this hidden pain later in my life.

REUNION AND NAVIGATING CHALLENGES

One day, I returned home from school to see Mother smiling and excited. Today was the day Father would return home from the hospital, she said. At first, I felt really uncomfortable with this news. The troubled thoughts returned: "What if I cry when Father arrives home? What if he finds out that I'm afraid he'll die?" I experienced mixed emotions of excitement and fear.

When Father slowly walked through the door of our house, he was smiling. Father had bounced back with resilience. He was happy to be home, and I was so happy he had returned. Alive.

We learned that Father had had a gastrointestinal bleed (GI bleed). The crisis had passed but his health challenges were not over, and soon, financial challenges would follow.

Mother was happy to go out into the workplace while Father remained home to heal. When he felt well enough to do so, he prepared delicious meals for the family. Human connection was present and gave me a sense of a safe space to grow in a nourishing way, even through suffering.

Although few in number, there were joyful moments when my parents would laugh, even dance, enjoying life in the comfort of our home. I remember Mother and Father smiling while waltzing in the living room, each one likely remembering moments of dance in Europe before collective trauma was magnified through the horrors of the Second World War.

When Father felt well enough, my parents occasionally went to a local Legion Hall to listen to a live band. There, they danced polka for most of the evening while socializing with friends. It made me happy to picture them smiling and feeling the energy of dance flowing through them, knowing that joy can be received despite our experience of trauma.

DEPENDENCE ON HEALTH CARE
AND GOVERNMENT

The transition from an independent, healthy family to becoming more and more dependent on the decisions of others was definitely a challenge. This burden that weighed down my father rippled out to all members of our family.

My parents had hoped to begin a new life in Canada. They wanted to bring more family members to this country and contribute to the economy, to society, to a new way of life for all. It was very difficult when a debilitating disease showed up and left them at the mercy of health-care providers and governmental decisions.

Unfortunately, Mother didn't earn as much as Father would have if he had been able to continue working, which caused additional stress from financial strain. Father felt shame and guilt, often telling us that he wanted to work but couldn't. He was well known for the hard work he had done in previous years and this had become a very difficult time for him. With Mother not making much of an income to provide for the increased needs of growing children, our family was moving closer towards poverty.

Father would often say, "You're only as rich as you are healthy."

My parents decided to ask the government for money. We were not only struggling with a low income but also Father's ongoing health problems. Eventually, we had no choice; we received welfare. Even so, I believe that even in hardship, there is always a choice – a choice of how we perceive what is happening to us. I felt gratitude that we were being helped by the welfare payments.

Along with welfare support came stigma. Many people had contempt for welfare recipients, believing many of them could work but refused to do so because they were lazy and they enjoyed taking advantage of "the system." This judgement was a symptom of the human need to divide, to label experiences and to put them into negative categories.

Father was well aware of the stigma and felt ashamed, and his shame was felt by many members of our family. Even though we needed this government support because my father was ill, it was a challenge for us to fully accept and appreciate the needed help. Although fully aware, I didn't absorb the stigma so much but instead, was most concerned about how my father was feeling.

Father was interested in politics, and he knew that decisions on where governments directed help to citizens depended on who was elected. One day, Father got an idea. He asked if I would write a letter to our Liberal Member of Parliament (MP) to advocate on behalf of my parents and to help the politician better understand families like ours who faced hardship, mainly due to illness.

Although I was a young adolescent, I agreed to write the letter. I explained how our family suffered from financial strain, a language barrier and my father's debilitating disease, all of which were adding to our struggles. It was very important for Father to have a voice, and to help people understand that he really wanted to work but couldn't. I had become his advocate for a short time.

A number of days later, I noticed a smile on my father's face. He had received a response from the MP's office, an acknowledgement of the communication. He congratulated me on my writing and said my letter helped. I had a happy feeling inside my heart when I heard my letter made a difference in the lives of my parents.

Our circumstances hadn't changed, but a doorway to empathy seemed to be opened.

Something very powerful happens when the voice is simply heard.

DEEP LISTENING

The language barrier was also a challenge. My parents spoke a "broken English," with a heavy accent, and other people didn't always understand what they were trying to express. At the same time, my parents often struggled to understand the language used by health-care providers and officials from government agencies.

I've often noticed, even today, that when someone speaks English with an accent, many English-speaking people, without conscious malice, often fail to take the time to really listen to the words wanting to be expressed.

I've learned our perceptions about ourselves and others are not always what we think. In this misunderstanding, we cause a lot of needless pain and suffering, often leading to or exasperating an existing illness – on a larger scale, even leading to conflict and war. Deep listening allows us to return to the present moment, where we feel heard and seen, and where we suffer less.

The feeling of not being heard or understood during a time when empathy and deep, compassionate listening were most needed caused more suffering for my parents. They were in a vulnerable position where their needs were not always met. They could only hope those making decisions on their behalf knew what they were doing.

One day, I could really feel the pain of my father's concerns. Basically, he didn't feel heard or seen and felt that no one understood what he was going through. He said, "They think I'm lying."

Thinking back, the frustration of not being seen or heard likely turned into an inner dialogue of negative thoughts in my father's mind, which often showed up as grief, sadness, shame and depression. These negative emotions release stress hormones into an already compromised immune system in the mind-body, which further contributed to his poor health.

Father tried to remain strong, but I could feel the depth of his feelings of hopelessness and helplessness. "I want to work. I can't. We need help." He repeatedly shared his feelings of isolation. "They don't understand us."

DISEASE

I later learned the full extent of my father's health problems. I found out that he had back surgery after a tree fell on him during his time working in the bush. One day, he lifted his white t-shirt to show us the scars left behind on his back from this operation. He also had eye surgery and this contributed to his inability to drive a vehicle.

And one of the most challenging surgeries had been to remove three-quarters of his stomach. This had occurred several years before his GI bleeding incident. One of Father's doctors later said that the operation should never have happened. During the surgery on his stomach, the doctor had mistakenly cut a nerve.

Father, like many, would occasionally purchase and drink alcohol. It was socially accepted and many people would drink a few drinks to get some relief from life's struggles. As we recognize, alcohol poses risks: numbing pain by drinking often makes the life situation you are trying to relieve, even more difficult. And of course, some people become addicted.

Perhaps fortunately, my father could not drink too much due to his reduced stomach. After having a couple of drinks, father would often miss family and friends from his home country of Switzerland, and in his nostalgia, he would yodel. One time when I was studying for an upcoming exam, I couldn't concentrate while my father sang traditional Swiss songs and then began yodelling. Not funny at the time, but it's a good chuckle and a happy memory now.

One day Father was in the parking lot outside the grocery store when he fell ill to the ground. It seems that some people mistakenly took him for a drunk and kept their distance, before one kind soul moved beyond judgement and called for an ambulance. Although not certain, Father had experienced a seizure, likely due to low blood sugar.

CONDITIONED TO SEPARATE OURSELVES AND TO SUPPRESS OUR VOICE

By the time I reached high school, I was pretty much conditioned by my parents, teachers and society, who were conditioned by those before them. We all received indirect and direct messages about what was right or wrong, good or bad, smart or stupid, accepted or unacceptable behaviour in school and life. At the same time, I carried layers of invisible childhood family hardships, intergenerational traumas and experiences in my life situation that had never been expressed.

In high school, it was all about the intellect, the thinking mind. Just like a robot in a controlled environment, I continued to obey all rules. I was rewarded as the good girl for doing it "right."

I quickly learned that anyone who finished a test in school first was fast and therefore, smart. One day I was the first one to hand in a math test and the teacher marked my test in class and told everyone who was still writing that I was the first to receive 100 per cent. I was proud to have my achievement recognized in front of my classmates, but I also felt bad for any classmates who might be struggling.

If someone was doing it right then the other must be doing it *wrong*. The right one must be *smart*, therefore the wrong one must be *stupid*. I was aware that I was smart in this moment but knew I could be stupid in other moments.

It was a continuous play of sizing one another up to see who to accept and who to shun. This human experience further contributed to human separation.

I noticed whenever emotions surfaced, we were often hushed by adults or ridiculed by our peers. When we expressed emotional pain, it wasn't always honoured. Instead, it was a sign of weakness, of fear. Whenever joy was expressed, there were comments from peers like "who do you think you are," as if we did not deserve this shared happiness.

I learned to further suppress my emotions, to swallow them, just like I had done after my father's bleed.

I naturally connected with my peers whether one-on-one or within groups. I've always had an underlying hunger for connection to everyone.

There were times when I unconsciously modelled a false sense of self to protect myself while trying to fit in. This included moments when I would cut myself down in order to help another person feel better about what they were going through. Afterwards, I berated myself for being ungenuine.

In school, some of us were loud in what appeared to be a desperate need for attention, to be seen, to be heard. Others were quiet. And some coasted along as if they had it all figured out, at least that's how they appeared to me in the external world.

I often questioned, "Why do I always have to be so kind, so understanding of everything? Why can't I get mad?" I continued to try to find my place to fit into this competitive world.

I questioned, "Where exactly do I fit in? Which direction do I take where society will accept me in school, in life? I just want to be me," as I continued to search outside myself for answers.

When I look back, I'm not surprised that adolescents have a difficult time trying to fit in. Whenever I looked outside myself for solutions, I shunned the inner self that I am.

In doing so, I began to wear an invisible mask covering up who I am, in order to do what I thought others expected me to do and how to behave. It felt like I had to always be on my toes to avoid being judged, in doing it the right way. It felt more like being moulded to become robot-like due to the decisions of those before us.

I silently questioned:

Do you accept me?

Do you like me?

Am I doing it right?

Am I doing it wrong?

Am I fast enough?

Am I too slow?

Do you see me?

Do you hear me?

Do you feel me?

Do you love me?

… the way that I am.

It was a constant struggle: I don't want to be what others want me to be. I just want to be me.

I wondered where human connection is in all of this division of opposites? When I felt I wasn't given the space to deeply make human connection with others, little by little, it felt as if I was not able to express my true self, my uniqueness.

There were moments when my mind would get entangled in thoughts of the past, leading me to sadness; other times, I'd become slightly anxious as I stressed myself predicting outcomes in the future. All the time I was avoiding the present moment because it didn't seem to matter. Whenever I became aware of fearful thoughts in my mind I went deeper within my heart space, naturally connecting to a calm state of being where there is *no thought*.

To get some relief from what seemed to me to be unexpressed emotional pain, I noticed many would complain, gossip, blame, compare, and even bully one another in a desperate need for attention in the external world. I shared some of my own complaints as I blended into the fabricated stories of the ego. Taking sides and judging others did bring relief, if only for a moment.

Although I blended in well, within myself, I was trying to figure out this thing called life, all the time questioning "where do I belong?"

No matter which direction I would take there was a constant play of opposites where I would have to put myself in a position to not be who I am.

I would find out later that the inner Self would guide.

Parties were fun times to connect with my peers. Alcohol, drugs and sex were always available to explore whether we chose to or not. I remember having fun when my friends and I drank enough to feel the effects. The joy from our laughter and conversations was more intense, somehow. It was a release and a conduit for many to feel more at ease and comfortable in our own skin. As long as I remained centred, I could be a little bit more of "the real me."

I would later learn that in adulthood, many of my peers would become dependent on these external temptations, which prevented them from processing their emotional pain and led to embarrassment about their behaviour. Living a false sense of self in order to please the conditioned, external world, these often embarrassing moments may have compounded, resulting in feelings of guilt and shame.

I didn't feel like I had the freedom or a safe space to openly express my unique self, without someone judging me, as I likely did with them. Whatever came to the surface to express itself, I would swallow it down to suppress. I became more and more constricted within and without, at times, kind of frozen, blocking the natural unfolding of who I am. I knew there was a missing piece to this puzzle.

Looking back, I know that over time I learned that the space between the words of opposites like good and bad, right and wrong, strength and weakness, positive and negative, even connection and separation, is a doorway in union with the higher Self.

It's my responsibility to go deeper within to observe and embrace this conditioned division in what it has to teach. Whether it no longer serves me or has never served me, I recognize this division of opposites. In going deeper within to the realization I am not who I have been conditioned to *think* I am. Through this recognition, I am connecting to the inner light that I am, living in action from my unique purpose for all, supporting others in human connection so we can grow and evolve together.

FIRST DEATH

The first death that I experienced of someone in my age group was that of a young student who attended our high school. All students and staff in the entire school stood up in silence to honour this handsome young man who had died and left his body at a young age. I felt sadness for the loss of a fellow student, his family and friends. For a moment, there was no pressure to have to be a certain way. I felt a depth of inner peace in connection to all as we came together in silence, in Oneness.

Society often sends messages that physical death is the worst thing that can happen.

There was no division; it felt so peaceful, so healing, if only for a moment. Afterward, we continued on with the daily activities of school life where separation, complaining and blaming continued along with the excitement of learning various subjects, participating in sports and making after-school plans with our friends.

I learned something during this very simple act of respect of honouring a fellow student. When the entire school stood in a moment of *silence* as in prayer and song, it connected us to one another. This was very familiar and something I was so comfortable with. Deep within, I knew there was hope for us to come together.

What if the unique purpose of this young man was to awaken us to go deeper within?

Throughout the coming years there were more deaths in our community. Whenever there was a transition, although I felt sadness, I continued to feel a sense of inner peace and often questioned how I could feel so comfortable at someone's funeral, while the experience was understandably very difficult for many. At times, amidst the pain and loss, there was joy and laughter, as the happy memories surfaced in conversation. Hearing of the death of someone took me from the chatter of my mind to my heart.

People would actually stop complaining about their life situation to hold space for anyone to openly share heart-centred experiences of the loved one and remain in a respectful silence. This resonated with me and was always so beautiful coming from the hearts of so many.

This was the inner peace I felt and continue to feel in the human connection.

I worked hard to obtain the credits needed to complete high school, and I finished school five months early within the first semester of the final year. With a curious mind, I travelled to Europe, connecting with loved ones, languages, cultures and countries that until then I had only heard about. Then the time came for me to return home to graduate from Grade 12 with all of my friends and classmates, many of whom had thought I quit school.

I walked away in freedom from the many years of being immersed in the education system, beginning in childhood and on into adolescence. I left this beautiful community of family and friends and went out to further explore the world.

I remained an unchanged silent witness open to the mystery of what is trying to get my attention within a continuous flow of change, where divine intelligence would guide.

A new chapter had begun.

Part Three:
REMAINING OPEN TO THE MYSTERY AND TRUSTING MYSTICAL KNOWLEDGE

"I do not fear death. I had been dead for billions and billions of years before I was born, and had not suffered the slightest inconvenience from it."

Mark Twain

"You can't bury me because you can't find me."

Socrates

Our intellect certainly helps us to reach certain goals in our world. But I have learned that our knowledge and experience are not enough on their own and over the years, I have increased my reliance on spiritual wisdom, allowing myself to be guided by a higher intelligence that may defy rational explanation.

I have received many signals that can be defined as "mystical" – premonitions or signals about events to come or greater truths without empirical evidence. They have come to me in various ways: a whisper, a tap on the shoulder, a word; in my sleep, in my body, a deep knowing that I cannot doubt.

I've learned that what I *think* will happen isn't necessarily what happens and what I *think* I should do isn't necessarily what I am to do. In holy presence, I do whatever I am called to do.

For the longest time, I refused to receive this cosmic intelligence that exists beyond the thinking mind. I didn't share my experiences with others, conditioned as I was to believe that only my mind digesting facts was the acceptable way to find answers.

I believe that mysticism has been treated as a joke for far too long. Looking back on my childhood, I realize this is part of the reason I remained in silence. I suppressed the Real Truth of who I am from coming through, not who I have been conditioned to believe I am.

Trusting mystical knowledge also allowed me to accept the loss of a beloved family member, to see that physical death is not the end of our connection with each other.

THE MIRACLE OF A NEW LIFE

The first time I understood the real meaning of the word "miracle" was when I gave birth to our first child, a daughter. It was pure joy beyond words, not only to my husband and me but to our parents as well.

One day Mother and I, and our now 17-month old daughter, were outside enjoying a beautiful summer day when my daughter picked up a yellow dandelion from Mother Earth. I watched her from a distance as she walked over to Mother, her grandmother, and offered her one flower of this beautiful plant. With a bright smile on her face, Mother graciously accepted this gift.

It was a precious moment to witness a divine connection between my child and my mother, the flow of energy in giving and receiving.

NEW HOME

My parents lived in a home with a long set of stairs from the living room to the bedroom. As Father's mobility decreased, he could no longer safely navigate the stairs. Frequent doctor visits had become the norm for both my parents, and it became clear it was time for my parents to move to a place with fewer physical obstacles and where they could get more support.

Years earlier, their names had been added to a waiting list for a seniors' residence, so it would be available when they needed it. Now, with the help of their family doctor, my parents were able to secure a one-bedroom apartment in the residence.

Mother and Father were excited but also somewhat anxious, especially Mother. She had become tired of moving from house to house throughout the years.

Their apartment was new and quite lovely. There were no stairs, of course, and it had a kitchen, living room, bedroom, washroom and balcony. The amenities in the building included a lounge to gather, convenience store, hairdresser, restaurant and a chapel. Mother and Father could walk out of their apartment and enjoy the amenities without having to go outdoors on a cold winter's day. Once they got settled and adjusted to this new way of living, my parents were clearly happy and relieved to be in a safe space.

I recall one visit where I could see how well they were adjusting and getting engaged in their new lives. Mother had something to show me, and she was excited. When she was younger, she owned a pair of black pants adorned with white polka dots. She loved those pants and ordered a similar pair. The package arrived and when Mother opened it – surprise! The package contained a short mini skirt instead! We exploded in laughter. I was so grateful to share this simple but joyful moment with my mother and to see her thriving.

It was all the more precious when considering what was soon to happen in our lives.

SIGNALS FROM DIVINE INTELLIGENCE

It was March of 1991, and my husband and I, along with our two-year-old daughter, were vacationing in Nassau, in the Bahamas.

And my young family was growing; I was close to beginning the 8th month of my pregnancy with our second child.

Many memories stand out for me about that holiday. One was the ocean water – the most beautiful sparkling, turquoise-coloured water I had ever seen. It stunned my senses, and I wanted to find a way to preserve the beauty and to be reminded of it in the middle of Canada's cold winters back home. So, I purchased a tiny bracelet with turquoise stones that evoked the pristine waters surrounding this paradise island.

I remember the warmth of the local people, so very welcoming with their uninhibited bright smiles. A smile, a beautiful universal language understood by all. When we arrived on the island by boat and disembarked, a Bahamian woman called out to my daughter. "Hey pretty girl, Bahama braids?" I connected with the woman's eyes and immediately thought it was a grand idea to accept her offer. I was amazed at how quickly the woman beautifully braided our daughter's hair and decorated it with colourful Bahamian beads. To be a part of the human connection between local people on a tropical island and our Canadian family was so precious.

Most of all, I remember a dream I had while we were on the trip. I dreamed that my mother had died. I couldn't help but ask, "Why would I dream of my mother dying when it was my father who was ill?" Mother had inner strength, a depth of silence and a profound presence. She was the primary caregiver, the glue that kept everything working together in harmony, and I couldn't envision our family without her.

I took a moment to ponder this dream before letting the thoughts around it dissipate. After all it was just a dream, and I didn't have to believe it, right?

Ten days later we returned to Canada.

Afterwards, while visiting with my parents, my mother told me that her wristwatch had stopped working, and I offered to help her get the battery replaced the following week. My mother and I had also made plans to attend a fashion show being held at our local art gallery.

It was April, and the day had finally arrived to attend the fashion show. I drove my vehicle to pick up Mother at the entrance to the building of her new home, where my parents had now been living for three months. With an inner glow, she looked as beautiful as ever.

When we arrived at the art gallery, we found a place to sit, placed our belongings on the chairs and strolled around for a few minutes to enjoy the beautiful space before the event would officially start.

I couldn't help but notice my mother was a little off. She wasn't her usual self, and it felt like there were brief moments where she was elsewhere, mentally. The event would soon start, and it was time to return back to our seats. Suddenly I felt something happening within me that is hard to describe.

As we walked back to our designated area, I told Mother I would join her soon. I decided to go into the public washroom to remove myself from the activity of people while attendees were settling down before the fashion show would begin.

The washroom was empty. I was in my eighth month of pregnancy, almost due to give birth. I remained calm and centred as I stood alone with my back up against the wall. Something mysterious was happening that I had no words for.

It was happening both within and around me. I felt it in my heart, head and gut but also outside of those limits. Everything was alive, lit up, vibrating within and beyond my body.

With an inner knowing that my unborn baby was safe, I embraced the mystery. I took a few conscious breaths, once again questioning, "What is it? What's going on inside me?" Although I was open to whatever was happening, I became aware that I had to be careful because I was pregnant, and I shouldn't be alone in the washroom for too long, especially like this. I took a few more conscious breaths before returning to Mother and sat down beside her before the fashion show began.

I would later have this type of intense experience again and discover that it was a connection with a higher realm – a signal that forces were shifting beyond my conscious awareness. It was mystical knowledge, but the message I received on this evening would only become clear in hindsight.

We enjoyed a beautiful evening watching the models walk up and down the runway. Afterwards, I drove Mother back to the entrance of her building to drop her off. Before she got out of the vehicle, I offered her a few magazines that I had already read. She usually accepted my magazines with a smile on her face, but on this night she turned down the offer. It was definitely out of character. I found myself thinking that she was still tired from the move and recognizing that it would still take more time for her to fully adjust.

I reminded her that I would see her the next day to accompany her to a doctor's appointment, and after that, as promised, we would go buy a new battery for her wristwatch.

As I drove from my mother's place, I looked forward to returning home for the night. Once home, I couldn't wait to go straight to bed. After a fulfilling evening spent with Mother, my unborn child and I were tired and needed our rest. Before retiring for the night, Father called to say Mother was not feeling so well. He had also noticed she wasn't her usual self. At that time, there didn't seem to be an urgent need to go to the emergency department at the hospital. I told my father I would address our concerns with Mother's doctor at her appointment tomorrow. We both agreed and said good night.

I was sleeping soundly when we were awakened by a knock at the door. It was about 2 a.m. My husband answered the door to find a police officer at the entrance way. The officer's face was sombre as he said my mother had fallen at home and was taken to the hospital by ambulance. He told me I was to call the emergency department as soon as possible. With my heart in my throat, I made the call and asked to speak with Mother's nurse. I could hear someone in the background whisper, "She doesn't know yet."

The female nurse on the other end of the phone told me that Mother had had a massive stroke and died instantly. I was quiet. I politely thanked her before hanging up the phone, taking a few moments to absorb the news I had just heard.

A profound depth of inner stillness, in silence, the word *Mommy* came to me, and I could feel it slowly dissipate. I placed my hands gently on my stomach, rotating them in a slow circular motion, subconsciously comforting my unborn child. I shared the news with my husband and we hugged before we called family members in Europe, then in Canada.

My thoughts were blank. I slowly made my way up the stairs back into bed where I lay my head on the pillow. I wondered, "Was this really true? Had my mother just died as I dreamt she would?" I thought about the previous night at the art gallery when I had sensed something was wrong with her. I thought of the moment I had my back up against the wall in the washroom, everything within alive and pulsating. It was as though I was showered in another realm.

I recalled the dream I had in the Bahamas. I thought about my mother's watch stopping and that time had literally stopped for her shortly after. Lying on my left side in the foetal position, I could feel the movement of my baby as we slowly fell back asleep.

I had received so many signals – clues from the knowledge that connects us all.

When we finally saw Father, he told us they had been in the kitchen when Mother complained of a sore head. In no time, she had collapsed to the floor. The force of her fall caused their small kitchen table to slide and then turn over. Understandably, Father was in shock after witnessing this. He too was thinking about all the years Mother had cared for him and their children with such dedication … and now this.

ACCEPTANCE AND HEALING IN DEATH

I stood before Mother's body in stillness, in silence. I gazed at her physical body – a body that had once carried and nourished me inside her womb, just as I was now nurturing the child I was carrying within me. Once a human vessel, Mother was now an empty shell that lay before me.

The body in human form once used as an instrument, a vehicle, a conduit, known by the name *Mommy*. Her personality, any thoughts or emotions, any excitement of her soon-to-be-born grandchild, plans for us to get her wristwatch repaired, the chance to wear the polka-dotted pants she had on order, her narrative, had all vanished. Gone. Just like that. And just like *time* had stopped working on mother's wristwatch, in a world of time, her human identity ended.

Yet, I knew the truth. Mother is nowhere but also everywhere.

In the days that followed, I thought about my mother's life. She had been the primary caregiver for us children as well as the compassionate supporter of my father and his increasing health-care needs. We all grew up and eventually left home as Mother continued to care for Father for many more years to follow.

More than 20 years had passed since Father's bleeding crisis, and Mother had also cared for Father in the years prior as he dealt with surgeries and disabilities. Mother had a whole other life in Germany prior to immigrating to Canada. I thought about the challenges she faced: war and the aftermath of war in a country that was no longer her home; walking away from loved ones to start a new life in a new country; and gut-wrenching separation in a divisive world. And yet, in all the pain and suffering of trauma, Mother returned home within and allowed her inner light to shine bright through service in action.

The conditioned concept of "death" I learned to fear, beginning in childhood after my father's health crisis, came from thoughts created in my mind through a conditioned society and not through the love in my heart. Standing before my mother's body, in meditation, I was deeply connected. It was a magical process and I came to the following realizations:

Death of the conditioned mind

Mother wasn't dead

Human identity died

Fear of death died

End of life died

Ego died

Mother merged into nothingness

Mother is nowhere

Mother is everywhere

Life is here, Life is there, Life is everywhere

Eternal Self, Eternal Life

I am Universal Love

I am alive

I AM

A deep inner stillness remained. I shed no tears.

At this moment, I knew life never ends as I was conditioned to *think* in fearing death. My fear of death died. I knew the concept of death is an illusion; it is limiting and could have easily kept me stuck in grief, but it didn't. Any attachments to the human role of Mother as I knew her, her human identity created by my mind, had dissipated. The physical body as I saw it would return back to Mother Earth, which is alive.

Mother is so alive within me right now.

This moment also confirmed for me that I am not who I've been conditioned to think I am. What remained was a knowing beyond words of the intellect. An infinite cosmic intelligence that is always available, where divine guidance flows through this human vessel.

Mother transitioned into a timeless dimension, leaving me with gems to discover.

In silence, the words arrived, "Mother, your story needs to be told."

NO REGRETS

Often, we don't know when a loved one transitions out of their human life. I now know we can receive messages or signals before it happens, as I did. And as I would become more open to receive what wants to express itself through me, I realized that at a deeper level, we do know. Also, the messages continue even after the transition of a loved one.

When Father called me, concerned about Mother, we didn't know she would have a massive stroke. As I reflected on this, I knew it was important for me to trust my intuition and know I had made the best decision at that moment. Rather than beat myself up about not making the "right" choices, given the tragic outcome, I learned that when living in divine presence with one another, there are no regrets. Surrender. I knew regrets are illusions made up in the mind. My true nature is divine presence, a sacred contract. When open to infinite intelligence, divinity guides.

I have come to know this intelligence never ever disappoints.

ARRIVAL OF ANOTHER MIRACLE

I was reminded of one of our conversations a while back when I had asked Mother what her favourite age was. With a bright smile on her face, she replied in German, "*dreißig,*" meaning age 30. Now I was the one who was 30. Mother transitioned while I was pregnant, just as Mother may have been pregnant when her mother was killed during war. Although in different years and circumstances, it is possible that both transitions may have happened in the month of April. Mother later gave birth to a beautiful precious baby girl in June, the light amidst the wound during a very dark time in human history – a miracle.

Many years later, although the expected date of my delivery was in June, in May, I gave birth to a beautiful, precious baby boy. Now, I had another miracle, another sacred gift. Our newborn son was in the nursery as I lay resting in my room. In silence, I released a few tears and felt them flowing down my cheeks. Mother as I had known her was gone for real. And although it didn't matter which sex our baby was, she had hoped for a son, a grandson. At the age of 30, I had the precious gift of a new-born son. How magnificent is that? Our hearts are forever filled with endless joy in the magnificence of eternal life.

While still in the hospital, one of the nurses brought my beautiful son to me for feeding. She had the exact German accent as Mother, and the nurse smiled at me and said, "He looks just like you." Rarely, if ever, would I run into anyone who had the same German accent as my mother. It deepened my connection to Mother.

As I held and fed my newborn baby, I noticed a photo of a rose hanging on the wall. I was quickly reminded of a sympathy card with a red rose a family member had sent to mark Mother's celebration of life. Roses are said to symbolise God's love at work.

With a blank mind and an open heart, I felt something within me shift again. I was much more open to knowing there is a higher power. I didn't label this power God because of the conditioned divisiveness around the word. I just knew I was connected. I knew I received divine guidance. I knew I held a miracle in my arms.

Not long after her transition, Mother came to me in a dream. She was a young woman with beautiful clear skin, dressed in white with white pearls around her neck. Mother was sitting in a huge banquet type of room, at a large round table with a white tablecloth on it. She was the only one at the table and in the room. Her hands held up at shoulder height, palms facing me with her fingers crossed, she smiled. She used to do this before I wrote an exam, her way of wishing me good luck and telling me everything would be okay. I had no doubt in my dream what her message was; she was telling me that everything would be all right, for me and for her.

What if the purpose of my mother was to awaken me to the holy presence that I am?

GRIEF

It's natural for us to want to avoid grieving and protect ourselves from the deep pain of loss. To our egoic mind, the departure of a loved one is a tragedy; it's unfair. How can it be that this person would leave us?

To me, grief is a portal, a gateway to my higher self, the part of me connected to divine intelligence. The attachment with my mother began when I arrived as an infant. It was during the disease crisis of Father where I naturally detached in connection to a higher Self, where I found an inner freedom. Even though my mother and I were deeply connected and very close, I didn't grieve much after her death.

I believe that I found peace with her loss because I didn't get caught up in the mind of guilt with thoughts like "I wish I had" … or "I should have," and other fabricated stories we wrap into our human identities. And when such thoughts did arise, with awareness, I embraced and honoured them and any feelings that flowed from the restrictive thinking.

Whenever I noticed emotions arising, I connected with the natural rhythm of my breath, placing my hands and focusing on the area of my heart with the words, "I am so grateful." In doing so, I was giving my emotions a universal hug. There were many moments when I wanted to call my mother to share my happiness. I was taken aback when I remembered she was no longer there to speak with by phone. "I miss you, Mommy." These thoughts and feelings would come and go, like the ebb and flow of the ocean waves.

There are no regrets, no guilt, no grief in holy presence.

Mother's death had been quick. Although there were *signals*, there was no time to say good-bye. But I didn't feel the need to say good-bye. I knew divine presence is everywhere. Even at this moment, I can easily imagine Mother sitting with Father having a discussion over a cup of coffee in their new home.

There were no tears but silence, universal love. I didn't have to fit in anywhere. I didn't feel alone and didn't question what I should be doing with these feelings.

I learned it's important to realize when living in divine presence with one another that we're connected to source. There is no separation. The beauty of "death" reminds me of who I am. Love, our essence. Real Love doesn't go anywhere and is always available, even now. Everything is as it should be.

Death of a loved one touches deeply. I was so close to my mother, and yet there was some mystical understanding that everything would be okay. I knew the concept of death does play a role in this human life of form: death of egoic thoughts, as I become aware of them and death of my attachment to the physical body, as it's absorbed into the living earth.

I die to the old every time I awaken to a new realization. I die every time there is a shift from an old, conditioned way of thinking to a new growth. I die to how it was, as I shift into the birth of something new, even if I don't know what that is, as the conditioned self slowly falls away. Precious gems, mystical gifts are ready to be discovered.

Part Four:
A CALL TO SERVE AMIDST THE DIVISIONS OF THE MATERIAL WORLD

"The best way to find yourself is to lose yourself in the service of others."

Mahatma Gandhi

"Life that I am, serving life that I live; life that I live, serving Life that I am."

Edith Alig Gagné

After I lost my mother, I was once again guided by higher intelligence. My inner voice was speaking to me and I listened – my purpose was clear. As Mother's soul transitioned into the mystery, a silent, sacred contract with Father was in the works.

In childhood, I was blessed to naturally connect with the absolute in the midst of my father's disease crisis. Becoming a witness, experiencing a depth of presence in the face of human suffering, is powerful in what can appear to be an overwhelming world of chaos. Living in presence to my father's next stage of life was once again what *I am to do*, where I was called to be of service.

My new contract: I would now support my father and advocate for his needs as his health struggles continued. Rather than worry, I shifted to concern for my father's health and well-being. The presence I had drawn upon as a child would serve both of us again as we struggled with daunting challenges and with the divisions that dominated the world of the material.

Even though it wouldn't always be easy for him on his own, Father chose to remain in his new home. I became his primary caregiver and took on responsibility for key decisions as power of attorney for his personal care and finances.

I stepped into the role my mother had occupied for all those years as an informal caregiver for my father, being his advocate within a health-care system that often failed patients and denied them respect.

My new mission would test me in ways I didn't fully expect, but it would also bring me deeper spiritual insights and lead me in new directions in my life.

ANSWERING THE CALL TO SACRED SERVICE – I AM WILLING

Flareups of my father's numerous health problems meant that we frequently ended up in the emergency department of our local hospital. In addition to his serious digestive issues, he had acute diverticulitis and diabetes and was often anaemic. Sometimes, these trips would lead to him being admitted for medical tests or treatment in the intensive care unit or another ward.

I learned to centre myself and remain in the present moment. Whenever my thoughts jumped to the past or into the future with fearful thoughts, I would notice them and return back to the heart-mind connection I had learned in childhood.

One day when Father returned back home, while coming to visit him, I was approached by a member of the facility's support services team, who explained that we could get extra help for my father if he needed it. Father and I both believed this would be beneficial, and we agreed to pay the additional fees.

I was truly grateful to this woman for approaching me. On his journey, Father met so many caring staff and that included many personal support workers. To get this additional help was a gift to us both.

My new role included supporting Father through his own grief. He was grateful to Mother for the many years she had supported him with grace and ease. He certainly missed her, but I knew he would adapt to her absence. It was important for us to create space for one another to share memories of Mother, telling stories of both pain and laughter.

I was aware that Father might not fully open up to me, a parent's way of protecting a child from any potential pain and suffering. Later, I heard of a volunteer who had come by to support Father on the morning Mother transitioned. God bless her. It was so important for my father to have someone who would create a sacred space for him to openly express his pain and sorrow, a space of healing.

I would combine the responsibilities I had for my own young family with not only the ongoing health-care needs of Father, but most importantly, our father-daughter relationship. I was devoted to his health and wellness, willing to be an advocate for my father on this journey we were on. With an incredible amount of patience, I was open to whatever came our way, without any expectation of outcome.

Devotion, known to be "the highest form of intelligence," an intelligence beyond the intellect, never disappoints and would transform everything on our path.

I learned emotional self-care was just as important as caring for my mental and physical well-being. I was more receptive, accepting and embracing of any emotions that arose in me.

Therefore, I never got caught up so much in the fabricated stories created by the mind. Instead, I continued to observe them and was aware when emotions like anger or sadness arrived. I knew these emotions would leave and return, only to leave and return again.

THE SEARCH FOR EMPATHY AND COMPASSION

I remember how proud I felt as a child when my father told me, "You could become a doctor someday." Of course, many parents deliver this kind of ambitious career message to their children, but I saw this as a special compliment, and I remember it boosting my self-esteem. Physicians have high status in our society, and I grew up thinking medical doctors were like God. After all, countless times, they had saved Father to bring him back to us.

Physicians, however, are still human beings who can get caught up in their own egos and find themselves entrenched in human-built institutions that shut off compassionate connection.

One of the first times I was confronted with this reality was when, as an adult, I joined my parents during one of my father's emergency room visits. Mother was always at his side, and I wanted to support both of them.

I remember that beforehand I was confident that Father would be well looked after in the hospital, and this would give Mother some relief. I envisioned how the scene would play out: She would have an opportunity to explain what had happened before she had called an ambulance, and the health-care team would graciously take over with empathy and compassion. At that time, I had full trust in professionals.

Mother and I were standing in the emergency room next to Father as he lay on a stretcher, when the doctor entered. Mother spoke in her deep, clear voice with her heavy German accent and explained what had occurred. Mother was an expert on my father's health, expertise earned through years of selfless service to support his continuous needs. A depth of presence and deep listening from the physician would help her during yet another difficult time.

After mother explained, we both looked to the emergency doctor for his professional response. The doctor then turned to me, not her, and looking exasperated, said, "I can't understand a damn word she said," before he stormed out of the room. I was literally speechless, dumbfounded by what I had just heard. There was absolutely no courtesy or respect for his patient's elderly spouse.

I looked into the eyes of my mother, the kindest, most loving and compassionate woman I knew. I could feel her sink a little deeper within herself, her face swelling right before my eyes. She took a deep swallow in an attempt to digest the inconsiderate words she had just heard. I can still see her face, her shock and emotional pain, now all a frozen memory in time.

My mother and I both remained silent. I observed my thoughts and my rising anger: "He stormed off! What?! How dare you? Did Father hear this?!"

It was another defining moment for me. My whole perception had changed; I would never again put the role of a doctor on a pedestal.

I knew this was not the first time health-care professionals had not understood Mother or Father. Father had often resisted going back to the hospital, and when I was younger, I hadn't understood why. Now, I have more clarity. Is this the type of behaviour my parents had been dealing with?

I imagined my parents, two elderly human beings in a vulnerable place, who had been a part of the health-care system likely while the doctor was attending high school, university, then medical school. They were dependent on professional advice and direction; their health needs were in this person's hands. An elderly couple had to somehow find a way to rise above this insensitivity in order to get their needs met during a health crisis in an emergency department.

I knew we cannot give what we don't have within. I was a witness to the suffering of my father, mother, doctor and my own. Suffering upon suffering among the roles of a patient, caregiver, daughter, and doctor – four fellow human beings caught up in the rippling out of disease and trauma.

I looked within to find compassion for this physician who had uttered such cruel words. I remained open to understanding his internal conflicts and stresses and to seeing him as a fellow human being who didn't know how to contain his emotions due to his own unmet needs.

As I supported my father for several years, I experienced more instances of indifference and insensitivity on the part of health-care professionals. When these lapses occurred, I fought for the rights of my father without hesitation, while also cultivating empathy for the doctors and nurses who were struggling themselves, within a limited system.

Although I was grateful for the care of many amazing health-care professionals, and they do exist, I began to slowly lose respect for the medical team as I continued to see with new eyes and listen with new ears. The added suffering of Father I had witnessed during my childhood was real. And now I understood where this pain was perhaps contributing to an existing entanglement of pain in dealing with the health-care team.

Empathy is needed to connect and feel the emotions in another. In doing so, having an inner desire to help not for our own benefit but for the benefit of all. This is really about the need for us as fellow human beings to come together through liberating the energy of compassion, allowing the essence of love, our true nature, to come through. Where compassion transforms suffering into Light. In holy presence, a depth of healing naturally occurs for all, even in the midst of a crisis, including in the role of a doctor.

It has been my experience that it is not only the roles of patient and caregiver that suffer but health-care clinicians like the doctor, as in this situation. This is not about *blaming* health care; it is about bringing *awareness* to the ignorance of not knowing the Real Self, thereby a reflection of human suffering rippling out into systems that no longer work.

In pure presence, solutions arise from deep within. In childhood, I learned to rise above the roles of the story played out before me. It is my wish during the release of inconsiderate hurtful words of a stressed emergency room doctor, a fellow human being, in the midst of the suffering of his patient and family, in the midst of his own suffering, that all receive healing in moments of inner silence.

EDUCATING MYSELF TO STRENGTHEN MY CAREGIVER ROLE

For me, self-care evolved into taking part-time classes at our local university to stay up to speed with what was being taught in health care. I wanted to expand my knowledge so I could offer Father the support he needed while also understanding the perspective of the health-care team.

I was not only a student; I had also been living alongside my father and had witnessed the effects of decisions that health-care practitioners made for suffering patients, for many years. What was delivered by these professionals and what I was taught as a student, didn't always match Father's needs as a patient, as we were confronted with more and more challenges along the way.

Father's illness was unpredictable, and he needed someone to support and advocate for him, especially when he couldn't. I had an inner hunger for some sort of information and understanding of not only how to meet Father's needs but to have my own needs met on this journey. This kept me grounded and moving forward in what I believed to be a healthy way. I not only challenged my mind at our local university; I also set an example to younger generations of the importance of education, no matter our age or life situation.

I leaned towards the areas of psychology and gerontology. I hoped that I would eventually have a professional career, so I could do my part in more of a conscious, collective setting to contribute to society. I was drawn to the idea of one day becoming a Doctor of Psychology. I didn't share the idea with anyone; I kept it as a private thought, an inner motivator. I was also interested in gerontology so I could meet the needs of my father, especially as he aged.

Below the surface there was this conditioned little girl who wanted to do it the right way in the external world, but I would soon find out life had other plans for me.

I would learn that although these roles and positions are needed, they were secondary to my assignment, my unique purpose. Cosmic intelligence spoke much louder than society's expectations of me.

ARRIVAL OF ANOTHER MIRACLE

Through rest, movement, nourishing foods and water, walking in nature, and even education, I maintained a state of balance where my well-being was reflected in healthy relationships. Benefits like happiness for no reason just showed up. Most importantly, I nurtured a healthy relationship with myself, which rippled out to others.

There were many joyful moments when I wanted to call not only father, but mother to share my happiness. One of those precious moments was when we became pregnant with our third child. I was so happy to share this news with my father. In the month of June, another miracle came into our lives when we gave birth to a beautiful baby boy, who blessed us with immense joy. A blessing, a precious miracle.

I can still see the big smile on Father's face whenever anyone said our newborn son looked just like him. He was so proud.

Although I didn't call it meditation or anything, for that matter, I lived a meditative life. In a state of homeostasis, a self-regulating process, I adjusted easily to a steady change of external conditions, where challenges and opportunities were continuous. I learned that when I focus on well-being, the benefits naturally show up. It was about living a conscious, healthy lifestyle in the moment, and not based on a short-term goal to lose weight, for example.

I was open to anything that would present itself at any given moment. Anything.

DIVISION AND EGO IN THE HEALTH-CARE SYSTEM

As I have described, during my childhood, my parents often expressed their disappointment at the lack of understanding from health-care providers. When I became my father's primary caregiver and helped him navigate the medical world, I had direct experience of this dysfunction.

When my father went to the emergency department, it was always by ambulance. We had been through this routine for many years, and Father would intuitively know something was brewing before calling me to let me know he needed an ambulance. We were a team.

As Father's advocate, I would drive over to be with him in his home or meet him in the emergency department. He would often say, "It's good that you are with me." When he was admitted to a ward, he told me, "The doctors and nursing staff act differently when family is around. They're more friendly."

Father was not the only one who was intuitive. On one occasion, my youngest son, who was five and a half years old at the time, was sitting next to me at the kitchen table with both elbows on the table while putting his face into his hands and said, "Mommy, can you save me?" Intuitively, he was able to express what was needed in that moment. Listening deeply, I took loving action and brought him to see a doctor, which led to him being admitted to the hospital with pneumonia.

In this direct knowing, intuition comes through a clear pathway with a higher vibration of consciousness.

At the same time, on the opposite side of our city, my elderly father was experiencing delirium and was also admitted to a hospital. Knowing of my father's concern to have someone by his side to advocate when needed, I travelled between both hospitals for six days. Each day, by way of divine presence, I was able to calm Father's delirium before heading back to spend the night in support of my young son with pneumonia.

There are moments where modern medicine can also be miraculous. I am grateful for many health-care professionals, in what education has to teach and in what science has to offer.

Nonetheless, I often found myself disturbed by hospital staff making comments in front of Father. It wasn't unusual to hear these types of complaints: "I can't wait to stop working at this place, to retire. I've got five more years!" Other times, many expressed their happiness that it was Friday, so they could escape for the weekend. Or how depressing it was that it was only Monday or that the weather was nice and they had to work. It was as if it was the worst possible place to be. I wondered if patients like my father were getting a message that they were a burden not only to family but to the medical professionals who were responsible for treating them.

As I observed this type of language, I felt it was inconsiderate of the patients, who were often in the hospital for long periods of time and trying to overcome complicated health challenges.

Rather than living in the present moment, I noticed that many of the complaining staff were not happy within themselves and waiting for something "out there" to make them happy. An unconscious habit, leaving us stuck in a repetitive thinking pattern of wanting to be somewhere else other than where we are.

Although I was disappointed, I made a conscious choice to step back from judgement, showing empathy to all and recognizing the lessons we can apply to our lives. One key lesson I live by is the recognition that I am not dependent on anyone or anything outside myself for my happiness.

It's not productive or healthy for us to give someone else responsibility to make us happy. Anyone or anything external can be taken away, but self-love cannot.

I also saw that staff would often blame one another without taking personal responsibility. I would hear nurses blaming other nurses, doctors or administrators for a specific problem, as well as doctors blaming other doctors and questioning their competence. Many times, they had good reasons for their criticisms, but the patient and informal caregiver were in the middle of it and that affected the quality of care. Poor decisions and mistakes were made.

There comes a time when an ill patient, who is someone's spouse, parent, grandparent, sibling, colleague or friend, surrenders to disease and puts everything into the trust of the health-care team, hoping they know what they're doing to deliver care. If the team is not functioning properly, it affects the patient, their family caregivers and all the members of the team. This contributes to needless pain and suffering, and it's not professional.

As a family caregiver, fatigue and feelings of doing it alone can put you in a position where you are reluctant to advocate. At times, I did feel too exhausted to stand up against health-care decisions I was concerned about, but sometimes I found bravery.

On one occasion, Father had been in the hospital for a few days and nursing staff told me they were ready to send him home. My father was still weak and barely able to get out of bed.

Intuitively, I knew it wasn't the right time for him to be discharged, and I could no longer be silent. "No, don't," I said.

My father was so weak. I asked the social worker on the floor if he could be kept a little longer to give me time to further address my concerns about him with the doctor. In good faith, I trusted her position to be one of understanding, to have empathy and be more compassionate. After all, didn't my voice matter, especially during a time like this? For many years, I had done everything I could to support Father along this journey, taking on responsibilities that helped make it easier for busy health-care providers to cope.

The social worker's reply was cold and dismissive. "This is not a 5-star hotel." I was shocked at this response; it felt like a slap in the face.

Where was empathy and compassion? I was a fellow human being, a long time informal caregiver, who needed her support. I needed the little energy I had to meet the increasing needs of Father, myself and my family. I needed someone – a team, a tribe, a community – to support my father and me through this journey.

Again, I tried to be compassionate towards her, understanding her own struggles. If we don't go deep within to do our own inner work, how can we give back from compassion and love for a fellow human being?

Caregiver burnout was beginning to sneak up on me and show its face. The social worker ignored my pleas, and Father was still very ill when he was prematurely discharged and sent home. Thinking back, I realize I could have addressed my concerns with someone else when the social worker rebuffed me, but I was so drained, so overwhelmingly fatigued.

The human division that begins in childhood and is reinforced through parents, education and society still comes to the surface in adulthood and in our places of work, our professional lives. Separation through the conditioned egoic self continues to play out as we play different roles. I noticed division continuing through blame, comparing, competing, and sizing one another up or down to see if they are good enough for us. Blame the management, the doctor, the other nurse, and then move beyond that to blame the family, blame the patient, blame the system. I've observed this pattern for many years.

Every now and again a sacred blessing is present, and the light of one human being ripples out. This is healing. The human being could be a member of the staff, a family member, a friend, or any visitor or a patient.

One example of the "light of one human being" was a conversation I had with a doctor in a walk-in clinic. When she asked me what has been happening in my life, I mentioned the global trauma healing I am a part of. I told her my mother was a WWII survivor in Germany and that I cried many tears of individual and collective trauma, even ancestral trauma, that had never been released. She replied, "We cry with you." This is the kind of human connection that radiates wherever we go that is needed in all walks of life.

Whenever I am aware that my thoughts, comments or actions are based on fear, producing an invisible division, I stop my unhealthy ego in its tracks. I immediately say, "I don't do that anymore." Rather than me and mine, us and them, I make a shift to "we." In this awareness I begin to change my mindset from one of separation to one of unity.

THE PRICE OF THE UNSPOKEN

Silence is a dichotomy. There is the silent presence we can achieve when we step back from the chaotic thoughts in our mind: the silence of meditation, connecting with the power of the universe in a calm, wordless presence.

Then there is the silence of the unspoken words in the face of pain and loss: my mother's inability to directly face the trauma of war and her refusal to speak about the darkness, and my own silence about my father's health crisis. I suppressed my voice as a child and I felt the impact years later. The words not spoken can calcify in the body, and unhealed trauma can cause us harm.

The fatigue began towards the end of my pregnancy with my second child. This was shortly after my mother passed away, and under the circumstances, I thought feeling tired was a natural reaction. I didn't think anything was wrong.

A few years passed. My energy continued to be weak and the decline increased after the birth of my third child. I felt more tired now than I had ever felt before. I thought it was the demands of caring for three young children as well as supporting my father's needs that made me so exhausted. I was concerned about Father's health, never knowing which direction it would take, plus I continued my part-time studies at the university. I continued to practise nourishing self-care, but yet, the fatigue didn't ever really diminish.

It got to the point where I literally dragged myself from one task to another. I had nothing left inside me, especially when I would have to use my thinking mind to contribute to discussions and assignments in all of my classes. I experienced a deep brain fog, and there were moments when I almost fell asleep in class, even though I slept all night. I would often question, "Why am I doing this?" A quick response came from my mind: "Finish what you started. Set an example." And so, I continued.

Not long after the birth of my third child, I was diagnosed with hypothyroidism, an autoimmune disorder where the immune system produces antibodies that attack the thyroid, and as a result, the thyroid gland doesn't make enough thyroid to meet your body's needs. The blood test they used showed that my hypothyroidism was quite severe. Fatigue is a common symptom.

I researched as much as I could about hypothyroidism and was in denial for an entire year. "How could this be?," I asked myself. I had led what most would consider to be a healthy life and practised self-care to prevent disease or ill health, pretty much daily. I recognized that prevention could possibly delay the onset of a disease, but it didn't necessarily mean I wouldn't be diagnosed with one. And so, along with my prescription for thyroid medication, I modified some of my foods and workouts.

Years later, I learned about the chakra system, which originated in India between 1500 and 500 BC in the oldest scriptures of Hinduism called the Vedas. One of the chakras, the throat chakra in Sanskrit known as *Vishuddha*, is responsible for communication, associated with speaking and expressing our personal truth. Closely connected to the thyroid gland, the throat chakra, when blocked, may cause issues associated with creativity and communication.

That's it! Of course, no one in the health-care system ever mentioned anything like this to me. It is focused on science and shuts off access to the inner science of spiritual wisdom. I was not surprised when I found out about the throat chakra and its meaning. For many years, I had deeply suppressed my voice. It was a relief to read this. This is an example of how we can learn from these ancient teachings, thereby bringing us closer to rise together.

It is possible hypothyroidism was the result of what I hadn't expressed, beginning in childhood and on into adulthood. Eventually, I was grateful that there was a medication for an underactive thyroid to help my body come back into some sort of balance.

My suppressed voice brought me back to childhood when I first entered school after my father's bleeding incident at home. I didn't know what to do with what I had experienced, and so I learned to gulp it down.

I thought about the suppressed voice of Mother, who had undigested trauma due to experiences of war and who wanted to "forget war." And then much later, she had to support my father through his continuous health challenges, a reflection of his own undigested trauma manifesting as chronic disease. This meant my parents were not always available to meet my often unexpressed needs in childhood and adolescence.

I quickly learned to be a *good* girl in school, bringing joy to my parents and helping to ease the burden of suffering within our family system. I didn't want to burden them further due to all the pain and suffering they already endured. In doing so, I learned to swallow the depth of silence of unspoken war coming through Mother, swallow the unspoken pain and suffering of disease I witnessed through Father, swallow any emotions trying to rise to the surface to express themselves.

When our voice is longing to be expressed, we must acknowledge, accept and embrace it and not swallow it back down.

My lack of voice, an underlying layer, would one day come to the surface wanting to be seen, to be heard, to be felt, and that time is now through the writing of this book. A diagnosis of hypothyroidism is one way my body and mind would try to get my attention.

I WANTED TO SCREAM AT THE TOP OF MY LUNGS

There was a moment in my life when I wanted to stick my head out the window of my house, face the woods and scream at the top of my lungs! Just scream as loud as I could. Aaaaaah!!

What would the neighbours think?

My suppressed voice was rising to the surface, wanting to be heard through the sound of a primordial scream. A powerful inner release was needed.

If I were to suddenly scream, I would scare my young children. Wouldn't I?

What do I do? Where do I go?

I thought of going out into the back field to let it all out. Who would watch my children? If someone were to watch them, what would I say? I need a moment to go scream in the field. What if someone heard me and came to the rescue thinking I was in danger? Would they get it or think I was totally crazy?

The increased demands of caring for my father while raising a young family with my husband, pursuing an education to work towards a potential career and maintaining my friendships left me more and more fatigued. I could feel the pressure of trying to meet the demands of society building up in my throat before swallowing it back down again. How could I work towards a career when drained and exhausted?

Caught up in the demands of life I no longer knew who I was. I surrendered to the question. Who am I?

My suppressed voice from my father's bleeding crisis and mother's toxic silence of the trauma of war had left a frozen layer still buried within me. The "good girl," I was there for everyone. This left me with no space to meet my own needs. With a diagnosis of hypothyroidism, fatigued with a lack of voice, I had nothing left in me to give out there.

And now my inner voice wants to be heard through the sound of a long powerful scream!!

Is this healthy? Absolutely!

Imagine screaming at the top of your lungs over a calm lake echoing out to all. This is healing.

Screaming releases the energy of pent-up emotions rising to the surface to restore harmony.

Intuitively, I was called to scream out loud while in my home with small children. Trying to juggle everything, I was caught up in the constant demands of society's expectations of how it should be. My physiology was trying to get my attention and show me that my inner and outer worlds were not in harmony.

Feeling lost, no longer knowing who I am, I returned to nature outside my washroom window. I moved from the chatter of my mind to giving voice to my heart. Alone, I made a few quiet scream-like noises, aaah, aaah. I began humming and could feel the vibration in my throat. Soon after, I connected with my young children through the sound of children's songs. Together in silliness, we moved our bodies to the rhythm of song, creating more space and bringing more balance in equilibrium. Thinking back, I could have easily had a moment with my children where we all roar like a lion. How fun would that be and could still be, with children and adults, alike?

It's so important to find a healthy way to express what has been suppressed for far too long.

RISING FEAR

"We suspect that your father has cancer. He is not a good candidate for surgery."

When I heard these words from the doctor on the other end of the line, I immediately noticed fearful thoughts arising, and my body became stiff and constricted. Not long ago, the doctors had found a large lump in my father's groin area. Even though the doctor wasn't definitive, I knew at a deep level that the cancer diagnosis was accurate. I was aware of my mind jumping in with jumbled thoughts taking off in multiple directions, due to fear.

I reminded myself that an unconscious society had unintentionally instilled fear in many people, including me. Just hearing the word "cancer" was the perfect example of fear-based conditioning. Becoming aware of this brought me back into the present moment where my fear of cancer slowly dissipated.

I was reminded of a recent conversation Father and I had had about death. We were sitting at his kitchen table when I asked him, "Are you afraid of dying, of death?" Father calmly said, "No." He continued: "It will happen soon. I can feel it." I felt peaceful when he said those words, and so did he.

Both my father and I had the ability to connect to an invisible *knowing*, a source of knowledge beyond and deeper than rational thought. It was a knowing within the unknown. He *knew* that his physical death was not far off without knowing intellectually what that would look like. We both trusted in this knowing and surrendered to the fact that everything would unfold as it should.

∞

Father had once said, "The face never looks happy when the body is in pain." I felt great compassion for my father for all the years of pain he had gone through.

Now in the wake of a presumed cancer diagnosis, Father's pain was becoming intense, and the doctors recommended that he take opioids. It took me back to a time, years earlier, when he had been prescribed opioids, and then one of his doctors told my mother and me that he had become addicted to the medication. The remark was almost offhand, and there was no further discussion on the topic. I didn't know if my father even knew he was prone to becoming addicted to this medication.

It made me think about how medical professionals sometimes prescribe drugs because they feel they're running out of options, even though there are dangers to the patient. I didn't think my father was well served by some of those earlier decisions.

Now that Father was again prescribed opioids, he spoke to me about the topic for the first time. He too had a new perspective. He told me the prescription pills he had taken a number of years ago have a purpose, to treat pain, and it is not wise to take them when it's not warranted. It seemed that he had come to a deeper understanding. "Before I took pills for the wrong reason. Now is the right time for pain pills."

ACCEPTANCE AND PEACE

Both my father and I continued with our sacred bond as his health continued to deteriorate. An ambulance was called not long after father had returned home on one occasion, and he was back in the emergency department, with me not too far behind. I arrived as I had done for many years and sat beside the bed he was lying in. There was always an incredible reciprocal feeling of inner peace between the two of us. An invisible knowing that whatever would show itself would be accepted.

One evening after visiting Father in the hospital, I returned home and laid my head on my pillow for the night. A few tears trickled down my cheeks. Although I rarely cried, the tears were a part of the grieving process, which I was very aware of. I could feel a shift happening within. When I returned to visit with him, he asked, "*Hast du gestern in der Nacht geweint?* Did you cry last night?" I replied, "Yes." Intuitively, he knew.

Father experienced more serious developments during his later days in the hospital, including an upper and lower gastrointestinal bleeding incident that took me back to the crisis of my childhood. When it first began, the nurse who was caring for him screamed and called for the doctor. I witnessed her fear while I allowed myself to remain calm and still.

Staff were attentive as they quickly moved Father into the intensive care unit. Through nine of eleven hours of his bleeding, I stood beside Father as I continued to assist him. Neither of us resisted what was happening.

In divine presence, a timeless dimension, the clock is not watched. There is no fear.

It was evening now, and understandably, Father was exhausted. I made a conscious choice that it was time for me to go home and rest. I made sure my phone number was written on Father's chart, and I gave the staff permission to call me anytime throughout the night, even if it was for something minor. A kind nurse would take over.

Thinking back to this time, I was truly exhausted. In this exhaustion were blank thoughts, which left me open to receive, and here, divine presence took over. I thought about how higher intelligence had guided me through the difficulties of that day. This intelligence has never disappointed me, no matter what challenges I have faced. Being a silent witness to disease is an opportunity to connect in presence, rising to a higher vibrational frequency that ripples out to all.

I learned there is strength in presence. It's empowering, where there are no worries.

It's time for human beings to be open, to surrender to the fabricated stories of suffering, to surrender to what conditioned thoughts have been telling humans for centuries. What I know for sure is that I am not my thoughts.

There is hope.

During another visit to the ICU, I was sitting in a chair at my father's bedside when I observed him looking past the foot of his bed. I noticed something had gotten his attention. He began speaking as if someone was there, but there was no one in the physical form of a body. In a quiet, calm voice my father said, "*Ja Mama, ich komme.* Mama, I'm coming."

In fact, I wasn't sure whether he said "Mama," which he often called my German mother or "Maman," which he called his own French mother. Perhaps, it was indeed his own mother. I knew it is very common prior to an impending death for us to meet with the deceased biological mother who carried us in her womb.

In presence, I remained calm and silent, fully aware.

REMAINING REMOVED FROM ANGER

The following day, I returned to the ICU to sit with my father as he slept soundly.

I was still taking a couple of university courses, basically to keep me included in some kind of potential career and to keep my interest focussed on something other than what I had been doing as a family caregiver.

There were many times when I experienced brain fog and deep inner fatigue, likely due to my hypothyroidism, along with caregiver burnout symptoms. On a couple of occasions, my exhaustion and feelings of being overwhelmed meant I had to withdraw from my courses and retake them.

Now that I was back in school, I had an exam coming up and decided to study at Father's bedside in the ICU, using the study sheets I had in my bag. With a blank mind, I looked at the paper I held in my hand, staring at the white page beneath the letters, numbers, blue lines, scribbles and yellow-highlighted sections. It wasn't going to work; I was depleted. I sat in silence staring a while longer before putting the sheets back into my bag.

After a while, I decided to gently wake up Father to let him know I had returned. As he slowly began to awaken, I could see he was filled with anger. It was directed towards me for having awakened him. I received an earful. I observed his anger and didn't take it personally, in the knowledge that he had just been through so much.

There are moments when nothing needs to be said. If now was the time for him to express his anger, I would create the space for him to do so, without judgement.

In that moment, deep listening on my part was what he needed.

My father was moved to a private room in the ICU and it was increasingly clear that the end of his physical life was approaching.

Fear and sadness are the conditioned responses to such developments in our lives. It's as if we become frozen, limited to the experiences of the physical body dying, the human identity dying, our *thoughts* continuously focussing on the fear of "end of life" *out there.* This may cause us to become depressed and anxious rather than remaining within holy presence.

I learned if we can accept and embrace it all, surrender to the unknown, we can realize it's not what we *think* it is. By living in the present moment, we merge with cosmic intelligence and are guided to remain open to mystical knowledge wanting to express itself.

To me, it's important to honour fear of the conditioned impending "death" as it arises, giving it a universal hug. The beauty of death is that I can die right now, even before the conditioned "end of life" arrives in my life and in the lives of others. In doing so, I arrive at the self-realization I am so much more than the body and mind. Die to the conditioned fear that has been created by the thinking mind and passed on, generation after generation, which brings pain and suffering.

It's important to honour my fear as it arises, for it has something to teach me.

It's not always easy. I may not even know what the lesson is at the time. I feel, accept and embrace the pain and suffering, in the knowing that it will dissipate and may return again. If it returns, I do the same until it eventually leaves.

I arrive at a cosmic understanding that has no explanation, no words. It just is.

In this room we had a private space, where family could gather. Father waited for one of my siblings to arrive and when he did, Father squeezed his hand. Every person in the room had come together in a sacred space. Whether voiced, through our inner thoughts or in a depth of silence, we all had an opportunity to say and be with whatever we were called to. Goodbye, thank you, I love you, or nothing at all to our father or grandfather. It was nourishing to the soul. It was a beautiful space to just be with what is.

FAMILY MEETING

A family meeting was scheduled where we all gathered in a small cosy space next to Father's room. The doctor spoke of the impending "death." I had the roles of power of attorney and power of personal care, but everyone was invited to participate in the decision-making. Family members all had an opportunity to talk about anything they wished to address.

I asked if Father could be transferred to our local hospice, which was located at a nearby hospital. The doctor replied, "Yes." This response meant so much to me. It brought trust, support, comfort and hope to us all that our father's needs were being considered, and we believed that this commitment would be followed through with empathy, compassion and love.

In this connection with the health-care team, we were heard and had the confidence that we would be supported during Father's final hours in human form – a healing journey that can be difficult. To actually have the doctor come from love and compassion from the one heart that connects us all gave me hope.

We knew we were in good hands. Or were we?

ICU TO WARD

The following day I entered the ICU and to my surprise, Father was no longer there. I was told that he had been moved to one of the floors. I was taken aback. What had happened to the plans to send him to hospice care? Had they even tried to make those arrangements? Nobody could provide an explanation.

No one could give any kind of rationale for what had happened. At the very least, someone coming from empathy could have taken a moment to explain. Perhaps they couldn't find an available hospice bed or they had decided it wasn't the best time to transfer him out of the hospital.

No matter what the reasons were, our family needed to understand the decisions that had been made. But staff in the ICU were sending us a message that our father was just another patient who was no longer their responsibility. So, go and deal with the people on the ward where he was now located.

I wasn't too happy with this news, as I was led to believe that he would be moved to hospice or at least an attempt would be made to follow through on our request. Nobody had even made a phone call to let us know Father was being moved to another floor. Such simple acts of kindness could have gone a long way.

The option of sending Father into hospice care was never brought up again.

Now we had to deal with the reality of the moment. When I walked into Father's room on the ward, everything was scattered. I saw his thin frail body lying on the bed with a full oxygen mask on his face. His waffle mattress, which he relied on to reduce his pain when lying in bed, now lay in a messy bundle on the floor.

The bed was on an angle and not where it normally would be, giving me the impression that he was quickly moved into this room before nursing staff would attend to other patients.

It struck me that the health-care system was not only failing the patient, as I had often experienced, but it was also failing the staff. The energy in the room felt stale, cold and heartless, an insensitive environment during a very sensitive time. Gripped by shock and rising anger, I burst into tears.

Yesterday's family meeting had actually given me some hope. Now it felt like we were part of a robotic, quick "to-do list." The family meeting – check. Move the patient – check. Receive the patient (if that even happened properly) – check. Our voice really didn't seem to matter at all. It felt as though staff came from the mindset of "just tell them what they want to hear."

I proceeded to the nurses' station to request that Father's waffle mattress be placed underneath him. The woman at the station said they couldn't do it now because the nurses were going for their coffee break. I paused. By this time I was so burned out as a caregiver and so disappointed with the attitude of the staff.

A long-time informal caregiver is in such a vulnerable place. When you're depleted caring for a loved one, you need support. And it can be very difficult to muster the only strength you may have left to ask for help. And when you ask and the answer is no, this depletes you even more.

My nervous system had experienced shock at home in childhood (my father's bleeding crisis), in education during adolescence (topic of war), government (stigma) and throughout my human life in the decisions of health care (ignorance and arrogance). The ignorance of not being open to receiving wisdom from a higher intelligence and the arrogance that it's not worth knowing are limiting. Once we go deeper within, we come to the realization that life is limitless.

Thoughts were flying through my brain. Wordlessly, I was pleading with these health-care providers: Now is the time to show what you've been taught and to demonstrate how you show up. For many, many years I have done what I could to help Father, to help the nursing staff, to help the doctor, to help myself, to help us as a collective team. Now with an impending "death," a transition, I need the health-care team to step up to the plate.

But the more I surrendered to receive support, the more I was crushed.

Staff stood before me like deer in the headlights. "My father's dying and they're going for coffee?," I asked. I noticed a familiar face behind the nurses' station. It was the same social worker who not long ago told me, "This is not a 5-star hotel." Speechless, I gave her a fatigued glare as if to say, "How could you?"

Throughout this journey, I've experienced poor communication, which ripples out to the patient and/or to the informal caregiver, affecting the needs and quality of life of the patient, the very reason we are all here. Again, a disservice to us all.

With time, I was able to take a wider view and extend empathy to the health-care providers caught up in an unhealthy system. I learned that nursing staff, doctors, even social workers, and informal caregivers all need support, just as much as the patient does. In doing so, needs can be met in a very sacred moment when we all come together in union, open to cosmic guidance.

This is not so much about me and the journey with my father than it is about all of us. If we continue to complain and blame one another, still stuck in our conditioned human identity, we get caught up in a fabricated, repetitive story. Something needs to shift to break this repetitive cycle, and it begins with us.

One thing I know for sure is we all need each other to heal and grow. Especially when confronted with suffering.

TRANSITION

Although very thin, weak and pale, Father looked much more comfortable lying on the waffle mattress, his cheeks slowly sinking further into his face. A soft-spoken nurse came into the room and asked if she could wash him. We said that would be fine and decided to all go downstairs to the cafeteria. Some family members went ahead and were already there when one of my siblings and I arrived on the main floor to join them.

Shortly after getting off the elevator and preparing to walk to the cafeteria, I received an *inner signal* to return back upstairs as soon as possible. No words, no thoughts; just a knowing. I felt an inner sense of urgency and rather than take the elevator, I quickly ran up the flights of stairs, with my sibling at my heels. When we arrived in Father's room, the young apologetic nurse quietly said, "I took off his mask to wash his face and he just took his final breath."

It was obvious to me that this young new nurse was given the job because many staff were afraid of "death" themselves. Perhaps they didn't want to deal with my anger, and beneath it, my own underlying pain. The young nurse said, "I'm sorry. I've never done this before." I calmly told her, "It's not your fault. You probably did him a favour." The nurse spoke from her truth. She didn't try to cover anything up and didn't tell me what she thought I would want to hear.

I am forever grateful for her honesty. This is healing.

The young nurse quietly left the room. It is my wish that she left with her inner light radiating out to all who suffer in her presence. Before everyone else arrived, my sibling and I stood before Father. Although his transition was known as a good death, where we had the opportunity to be present with our father to thank him and tell him that we love him, even if it was the loving action of sitting in silence by his bedside, his "death" was also a relief.

I touched his skin in various places. His feet and hands were cool, but his neck area and chest were warm. I remembered he would often say, "cold hands, warm heart." I kissed his forehead. "Thank you, Daddy." I experienced the beauty of a sacred inner space during transition – a veil lifted, fearlessness, a final exhalation, a formless dimension.

How beautiful is transition?

I learned fear and grief happen when we are too identified with our thoughts, with our human identity. It was a gentle reminder to accept and embrace any feelings such as sadness, depression, anger and denial that may rise to the surface. Any feelings of emptiness and numbness must be honoured.

A divine gift.

There were no tears.

I stood before my father's body. In silence, words arrived, "Your story needs to be told."

Later that day, I rested by the fireplace in my home, surrounded by our three sweet innocent young children sitting on the floor by my feet. Nearby was my husband, along with a few family members and friends. There was absolutely nothing left within me to explain anything, even to the children.

"No thing" left but emptiness.

I was drained. What remained was a pure inner depth of silence. More than 30 years had passed, and here I sat, totally speechless, empty inside. This journey had been going on since I was a very young child, as were my children now. My mother had not spoken to me about it and I had been a silent witness to my father's suffering then, my eyes opened to an inner vision where there were no thoughts, no tears. Where no words were needed.

And now the transition of my father connected me even deeper to the inner wells of stillness, a loud silence, an emptiness where all is as it is. Thoughts came into my mind, "It's the beginning of December. Christmas will arrive soon."

And just like the miraculous "birth" of a child, there was the miraculous "death" of a parent. The beginning of human form at birth, the end of human form at death, intertwined and merging together as one into nothingness. The role of Father, just like the role of Mother, had ended. Both were nowhere and everywhere. Free from adversities, where there are no roles, no names, no accents, no gender, no pain. Divine presence, our true nature, remained. Our very existence is a miracle.

There's more to this journey than the emotions of pain and suffering, which could have easily been a distraction to my unique purpose had I not been aware and played into the fabricated stories of the mind.

Both my parents had left me with gifts of wisdom. And just like Mother's message of holy presence, the calm in the midst of crisis, Father's message was one of hope and resilience, the ability to bounce back from adversity. How beautiful is that?

It's all Love.

I remained open to the natural flow of life as it unfolded. I accepted and embraced any grief as it came to the surface, and in doing so, transforming it into wisdom, a beautiful mystical moment.

I had a certain period of time to remove my father's belongings from his apartment before it was made available to a new resident. Afterward, I returned to personally thank the support services staff who had so graciously cared for Father during the previous 11 years. One staff member shared her feelings with me: "Don't think that we don't grieve for your father because we do." It was a reminder that pain and suffering also affect care staff, who, beyond their positions, are human beings too. We all need the space to grieve and to support one another in the natural flow of giving and receiving, and in doing so, transforming grief into wisdom.

I learned grief can also manifest itself physically. On December 24, the morning of Christmas Eve, 18 days after father had transitioned, I woke up in the wee hours of the morning with a sore right neck and shoulder, a place where I often carried stress. This pain lingered and wouldn't leave. Clearly, it was trying to get my attention. I slowly made my way to have a shower to get ready for the day. I ran the water at a higher temperature in an attempt to help my shoulder release the tension I was feeling.

Before I knew it, my husband was trying to wake me up as I lay soaking wet, naked on the floor. I had fainted while in the shower. I came to and after wrapping me in a towel, he directed me to the nearby bed. I lay down in silence, feeling the energy of my inner body. I watched myself as I lay still. After a while I wanted to get up, but I couldn't move my body. I thought, "Was this really happening? Let me try this again." I was aware of my mind making a decision to get up, and when I tried, my body wouldn't move.

I didn't panic. It was obvious my physical body needed to rest, and I gave myself permission to do so for a longer period of time. A couple of hours later, I was able to get out of bed, get dressed and continue with my day. In a crazy sort of way, it was as if fainting brought my body back into homeostasis, a state of balance. And just like a dog shakes it all off, I bounced back with resilience and continued on with my day in a state of calm.

After my father's transition, I fell a couple of times. My leg or foot just gave out. During one of my appointments, my doctor said I showed symptoms of multiple sclerosis. Thankfully, an MRI revealed all was fine.

I'm not the only one who has collapsed after the "death" of a loved one. Throughout the years, I've met other caregivers who have fainted after a family member or a friend passed away. This is a reminder that supporting the health and well-being of caregivers is just as important as it is for patients, family members and health-care providers. It is my wish that we come together in unity, regardless of our positions in health care or anywhere.

There are precious moments in life when I want to share my happiness with my parents only to return to the utmost gratitude for the lessons I have learned in hardship. I'm not so connected to the human identity of my mother and father, but to the pure light that we all are.

Part Five:
THE CALL TO SERVE THE WIDER COMMUNITY

"There is something in every one of you that waits and listens for the sound of the genuine in yourself. It is the only true guide you will ever have. And if you cannot hear it, you will all of your life spend your days on the ends of strings that somebody else pulls."

Howard Thurman

"This sacred flame we tend inside is in communion with the circle of All."

Hafiz

Where would my path take me now? I acted in service to my father for many years, connected to something so pure. I also knew the conditioned mind was all about the idea of external validation: am I to do what others would admire? After all, I had also educated myself to support my father and now had "credentials" that could pave the way for a position with some status. But I didn't feel called to do this.

Ultimately, I had connected to a much higher calling. It was a deeper knowing that didn't involve the human distractions of identifying with a position or title, of doing things "the way they *should* be done."

I continued to embrace and embody this divine intelligence I tapped into in childhood.

My inner wisdom guides me to be of service for the highest good of all. At first, I didn't know what form this service would take; however, guided by intuition, I listened for the answer.

UNIVERSITY OR UNIVERSE? DYING TO BE OF SERVICE

Getting closer to nature connects me with this inner intelligence. In nature, thoughts become less intrusive and I naturally feel open to a truth beyond thinking, eventually bringing this inner intelligence into daily life no matter where I am.

During a visit to the beautiful Gaspé coast in Quebec, I walked along the seashore. While listening to the sound of the Atlantic Ocean waves crashing up against the shoreline, I suddenly felt like I wanted to jump out of my skin. Just as a snake sheds its skin when it outgrows it, I wanted to shed mine too. It wasn't because I didn't like myself or the skin of my body; I wanted to shed the remainder of any unconscious, conditioned attachment to my human identity.

I centred myself and considered what would be the best use of the university education I had acquired. Initially, I had wanted to learn more about my father's health struggles and the healthcare system. I was also motivated to "lead by example" to show my children that it was valuable to pursue a career goal no matter your age or life situation.

However, the more I studied, the more I began to think my studies could lead to a career. This view was partly me responding to conditioned thinking – I thought I should do something important with this education; otherwise, it would be "wasted."

Despite everything I had faced in the many years of supporting my father, and then dealing with his transition, I had been determined to finish what I had started and to at least receive a degree of some kind. Although my fatigue was unbearable at times, I continued to put one foot in front of the other to ensure

I had something to show for my academic efforts. I eventually obtained an Honours Bachelor of Arts degree in psychology and gerontology, along with a certificate in palliative care, and I was just short of a certificate in dementia.

In order to make a difference in these fields, I hoped to work towards a graduate degree: a master's or higher. But as I envisioned pursuing additional degrees, I felt extremely fatigued. I realized I had nothing left within myself to allow me to continue. However, I noticed something so profound happen while I was caring for my father. In connection to a higher intelligence during the pain and suffering of a human being, I was not fatigued. In this divine presence, I didn't watch the time. Intelligence spoke much louder.

I honoured all that I had accomplished, but in the end, I recognized that something much deeper inside me was manifesting. I realized that university had been a stepping stone and not necessarily the path to my true assignment, my unique purpose.

I was breaking away from the remnants of attachment to society's expectations of what I am to do. Education as it was offered was no longer good for my health and well-being. It no longer served me. The medical, alternative medicine and encyclopaedia of health textbooks I had often used to guide me through my father's many diagnoses, were no longer needed to support him. Everything came to an end and died. It was the end of a chapter in this magnificent human life.

To me, death is not only that of the physical body and all its attachments to personal identity but also a continuous "death" that leads to a "rebirth." Throughout our human lives, we can die to old beliefs and patterns. In this death and rebirth that I was sensing, I was discarding what was left of the old fear-based conditioned patterns I had witnessed, not only within myself but also within the health-care system – shedding all the needless pain and suffering I had seen, all the struggles around fear, guilt and shame.

In expanded awareness, I learned to honour what it had to teach me. The voice speaking to me was the spirit of compassion and sacred action to alleviate suffering. My motivation was to be of service to the collective and to do so in a holy presence where there is no division between "me" and "you." I knew that I didn't want to serve in a system marked by a division between superiority and inferiority.

Every moment, I was dying into selfless service to the highest good for all. A shift happens; it's invisible; it's healing. It is a transformation from suffering to presence, and this shift from individual to collective ripples out to transform the world.

I remain open and receptive to divine guidance through presence.

Shortly after Father transitioned, I saw an advertisement in our local newspaper, inviting people to sign up for training to become palliative care volunteers. Maybe I was the one who was to go to hospice, not my father. Maybe this was a way for me to dedicate myself to compassionate service with freedom.

Taking on such a role would be a doorway to continue to serve humanity. I said "yes" to this urgent inner calling, knowing that being of service was my soul's purpose. I had unknowingly prepared for this next evolution. The seed of selfless service had been planted many years ago, first with Father and now rippling out to the collective. Living most of my life observing, supporting and advocating for my father in his home and the hospital had created a receptive environment for this call for action.

Unfortunately, it would be close to a full year before the training would take place. If there was one thing I learned on this journey with my parents, it is the incredible amount of patience I had access to within.

I applied for the volunteer position and when the time came, I was grateful to be trained through a non-profit organization. A beautiful group of individuals had come together in the spirit of loving-kindness, and I couldn't ask for a better group to surround myself with. They were kind, considerate, loving and compassionate.

And yet, even in this environment, I saw signs of polarization and division. I fully respected everyone but knew change was needed.

The people who delivered the training shared valuable knowledge that I knew would enhance the care of patients. Information at the level of the intellect was important, needed and helpful, but at the same time, I noticed many of the presenters frequently referred to "us" and "them" – "us" as educated people with accumulated knowledge and experience – along with those of us who had signed up to become palliative care volunteers – and "them" as the clients and patients.

I would later find out "us" and "them" would at times include an invisible division between volunteers and those with positions of power. It is my hope that we merge for the betterment of all of us as a collective. In this merger, no one is superior or inferior to another, which includes the patient/client and loved ones. As one interconnected organism, we come from our true nature of Spirit.

Are we trying to apply our intellectual knowledge to fix "them," unknowingly creating more separation? When all of our focus and energy goes towards remaining on top in our positions of authority and likely believing that we're "experts" who know best, division continues, and we do a disservice to all. In my experience, in the workplace, many people are blind to our underlying divine presence. By getting in touch with our true nature, we have the opportunity to raise the energy and foster connection in our places of work.

I felt a responsibility to approach this volunteer work in pure presence to ensure the care I offered would never separate me from the client or staff. My longing for us to heal and grow together through our interconnectedness was put into action.

A depth of presence within suffering or within the impending physical death of a human being gives us an opportunity to awaken to oneness, opening ourselves to the mysterious magnificent intelligence that we are at our core.

I knew it was important not to ignore this divine intelligence that has been shunned and ridiculed for centuries. An intelligence so pure is healing for us all, even in the midst of a disease crisis, in hardship and during death of the physical body.

I learned I can't change anyone else. But I can change myself.

STEPPING INTO THE UNKNOWN,
OPEN TO WISDOM

In order to receive wisdom, courage is needed to walk into the unknown.

A level of depth, an inner knowing emerges where I am fearless and open to new insights. I have more clarity, with no pressure to use my energy to try to be somebody else.

I step into the unknown, rising in service as a divine channel to whomever I am called to.

Although I understood the reasoning behind the role of "palliative care volunteer," I didn't label myself as a volunteer or as anything for that matter. I didn't want to separate myself by identifying with a title. Sometimes people would make comments that fuelled such separation: "Oh, you're *just* a volunteer," or "How can you take on that role? I could *never* do that."

I released any attachment to these judgements. I knew if I identified too much with a label, ego could sneak in and take away from the real work that was needed.

If I define myself only by my position, I can easily put up a wall, a barrier, by dividing myself. I've often heard people who have retired say, "I couldn't say it then, but I can say it now," when referring to their hands being tied to be of service to fellow human beings in need. Rather than rising together, we end up unconsciously causing more suffering. I've experienced way too many patients and family caregivers suffering needlessly due to such barriers.

We must do better, be better, together.

Mystical knowledge wants to express itself through this intelligent human vessel.

An intellectual plan can be helpful to reach certain goals in our world. But without spiritual wisdom coming through interconnectedness with all, knowledge and experience alone are not enough.

By realizing who I am and what I am here to do, I know there is no turning back. I am forever grateful. I walk in sacred steps to the beat of the universe. In timelessness, there is no beginning, no end, no division, no title, no suffering, no death, no end of life. Ageless in a timeless dimension, I rise above the old, conditioned form.

When called to be of service, my human identity of a palliative care volunteer merges with the Real Self that I am. In union, I am motivated to assist by way of service for the highest calling. I have no fear of the concept of death or hospice or the sight of blood. I am open to whatever shows itself. When I am open to receiving guidance from divine intelligence, healing occurs.

EMBODYING MYSTICISM

Mystical knowledge can be difficult to explain because it doesn't come from the intellect. I had a dream that Mother, not Father, would die, and so she does. That was enough evidence for me to validate that I have access to mystical intelligence beyond the thinking mind.

I've never searched for this knowledge. It simply arrives. It's not something I try to learn to do; it just is.

Living in connection with this spiritual truth, I am receptive to mystical experiences even when I visit clients or patients in hospice. And I found myself having these experiences more and more as I continued my service, not only in hospice but in other areas where care is provided.

Throughout the years, I've learned mysticism just arrives, whether I'm in the presence of other human beings or alone. Once thoughts get involved, you lose it. However, we can remain grounded and centred and allow the mind to relax into a blank state, as I've done in hospice. In doing so, we tap into a knowing where a higher intelligence guides us.

I recall one particularly profound moment. Less than a month had passed since I first began volunteering. One morning while preparing to head out to volunteer, I was standing alone next to my large bedroom window.

Out of nowhere, just like a bolt of lightning, divine light entered into me – a truth higher than my personal experience.

The light came down through the top of my head, travelling down my arms to the tips of my fingers, down my spine, and down my legs to the tips of my toes. And as quickly as it arrived, it left. It went back up and out through the top of my head. Poof!! Gone. Just like that.

I sat on my bed and then went down to the floor onto my knees. I paused, and my mind became activated again. "What the heck just happened?"

When I have such mystical experiences, they come to me spontaneously. I am not planning or following anything or trying to be spiritual.

I continued to get ready before I drove to the hospice to be of service.

If you walk into a four-bed room on a hospice floor, you usually see patients in various states: some asleep, some resting with eyes closed, others with their eyes open. Curtains are often closed around the beds to give some privacy. But this time it was different.

Once I arrived on the hospice floor, I entered a room with four patients lying in their beds. The curtains and everyone's eyes were open. I stood for a moment at the entrance of the doorway, and something mysterious happened. I felt an instant connection to these patients, even though I didn't personally know any of them. A higher truth, in connection beyond this physical body, arrived.

At first, I saw the face of each patient staring back at me. The eyes of each person were glossy, and then a glowing sparkling light came through their eyes that rippled out everywhere. It's difficult to explain, but it was like I saw this all without using my eyes. In divine presence, it is the spiritual eye that sees, a vision that comes through the whole body as the human self merges with the light of cosmic consciousness – of Spirit.

There was no identification with names, gender, furniture or disease. No impending death, age, hospice or staff. No pain and suffering.

It is pure ecstasy in union with the divine. Pure bliss.

I felt called to swirl out of my body down the hallways into the nurses' station, in the presence of sentient beings disguised as patients, doctors, nurses, caregivers and housekeepers – whatever we call ourselves in our roles and positions in human form. A dance of pure joy overtook me. I didn't actually do this in the physical world, but I felt my soul and the greater power of spirit calling me forth – a pull to swirl in celebration, in ecstasy, embracing all that is. Life is so beautiful and so magical when we get out of our mind of thoughts.

This, on a hospice ward. A space built from a systemic culture conditioned to fear death and end of life. If there was any spiritual healing, it happened on a hospice ward.

TRAFFIC LIGHT

Driving back home from hospice, I arrived at an intersection before stopping at a red light. As I sat still in my vehicle, I had another mystical experience. With my left blinker turned on, I waited for the green arrow to allow me to make a left turn. Although difficult to explain, I will try to help the human mind understand.

My face faced forward the entire time. Suddenly, to the upper right (outside my physical body), a stream of faces moved in single file towards me. As if at lightning speed, they suddenly vanished as light continued to travel behind me, past the length of my vehicle. Then the stream turned around, travelling back past my face before turning to the upper right location again and out into nothingness. I could see it all without turning my head.

To explain further: in an instant flash, on an angle coming down towards me at the top right side of my face was a stream of faces flowing in a single file, in colours of black, grey and white; some had moustaches, hairstyles in a bun and different types of head fashion, like a top hat. At first they appeared to move very slowly in a sluggish way, like an old film projector. Then the stream of faces increased to an unimaginable speed – and became a raging river down a narrow path, with a glimpse of Mother and of Father in the mix of deceased people I had known, along with what appeared to have been ancestors by the way they were dressed. Everything intertwined as a magical mystery.

Before Mother transitioned, I received a mystical experience while pregnant in the washroom. At the foot of the bed of Father in the ICU before he transitioned, he was greeted by his mother or my mother. Ancestors were now reaching out to me through my work in hospice.

When the light travelled behind me, there were a few mixed visions of patients in hospice. Mother, Father and others who had transitioned in my life continued as if at the speed of light. If I were to describe the shape behind me, although not precise, it was similar to the shape of a figure eight, known as the infinity symbol, lying on its side.

My face remained facing forward towards the light at the intersection. I didn't turn my head to the right and back, and yet I could see behind me, not with my physical eyes but with the whole-body spiritual eye.

Then a quick vision of my body in my bedroom appeared. With my spiritual eye, a seeing beyond my physical eyes, I saw a vision of my heart outside my body, about an arm's length away and directly across from where my heart was internally located. And right below that external vision of my heart was a huge round ball of energy like a large fireball, swirling below in a circular motion, seemingly fully alive.

I felt the whole cosmos throbbing within me. A great calm.

It was an expansive, boundless, continuous flow of energy through giving and receiving. A willingness through the act of giving, curving out to be of service to my father, to be of service in hospice, returning back to me through guidance. My soul's purpose of sacred service. The energy of love, our essence.

The words arrived, "No one can love me more than I love mySelf."

It all happened so fast. Time to timelessness, form to formlessness. Poof!! Gone. I returned with just enough information for the human mind to grasp something to share with anyone who was open to a divine intelligence beyond the physical body. The flashing green light with an arrow appeared. I turned left and continued driving home.

Afterwards, the ego crept in with thoughts like, "What will people think if I tell them?" I knew mysticism *must* no longer be kept quiet. It is my truth, the Real Truth. I watched as my thoughts tried to make it into something it was not. I remained the silent observer. Grounded and centred, I remain unchanged in constant change.

Like for Mother, like Father, the words arrived: "Your story needs to be told."

Divine truth guides us through a world of division. In search of something more, we yearn to be seen, to be heard, to be felt, to be honoured. I embody, speak and celebrate the pure Truth that I am. This is Truth for all.

I have learned that suppressing this Truth has caused so much pain and human suffering in the world. I can access this Truth.

Through this very suffering, lies an opportunity to receive the messages waiting to be discovered. It is my responsibility to answer the call in what I am to do. No one can do it for me. As I move through suffering, an opening arises to the magnificence that I am.

Love, the universal love that I am - I love you for all that you are.

There is hope.

WALKING IN SILENT SACRED STEPS

Open to a deep inner knowing, a message in the mystery arrives. An action that I am to take. I never know the reason, even when I *think* I do. All I have to do is take action when guided to do so. Guidance flows through this human vessel. I've come to learn this calling never disappoints. Everything, everyone, shows up.

No need to impress anyone
No need to follow anything
No need to look for anything
No need to try to be anything
No need to feel like I know everything

The mystery I seek is seeking me.

There can be a beautiful vibrational energy of love and compassion on a hospice floor.

There were times when I could feel the pain and suffering of not only patients/clients/caregivers but many staff in health care.

As I continued my service in hospice, I found myself increasingly tuned in to mystical knowledge, and through this easy flow, I received more signals that someone would soon transition or had already done so. Sometimes, an inner knowing arrives in presence with the other person, but often, I received the message when the person was not near me.

After passing away, many have arrived in my sleep with messages for loved ones. Just like the message of Mother's transition had come into my dream, I received other messages that were for me or for a loved one of the deceased. One was that of a handsome man standing at the bedside of his beautiful wife, now a widow, as she lay sleeping. He had a smile on his face while he observed her sleeping peacefully. Another was a young man sitting on a rocky cliff in the sunshine near the ocean. Smiling, he waved his hand as if to say, "I'm okay." And yet another was a beautiful woman sitting at a table with the message, "Stay strong."

When I received messages while I was awake, whether I was in hospice or at home, I would feel a strong vibrational pulsation within my body, rippling out. It's similar to what I felt in the art gallery before my mother transitioned years ago. There were some moments when I would feel really ill within, which translated to an inner knowing, beyond the mind, that someone was ill or about to transition. In the moment, I didn't always know who specifically it would be, but it was someone I knew or had interacted with at some point.

When I later learned that a person had passed away, I would realize I had received a signal within a few hours or a few days of their transition. It's like I'm tuned into a radio frequency channel, and through that channel, the person is letting me know what is happening and saying goodbye. I may be guided to pass on certain messages to their loved ones, which I have done.

How wonderful would it be to openly share these mystical experiences more broadly, expanding this knowledge to everyone? But except when I had a specific message for a loved one, I kept my experiences of these signals to myself, silently questioning, "Why is this happening to me?"

At first, I tried to ignore these signals by pushing them away. But they continued to show up, happening more and more frequently. Signals, messages and synchronicities were getting stronger. Photos, whispers, a knowing, a feeling, including hospital patients I had met in person, acquaintances I knew in my younger years, and others who had all transitioned.

Signals sometimes reached me through technology, like my laptop or iPhone, where a photo or message would just show up, as if in error. A couple of people whom I met online through various groups of study became palliative, without me knowing. One had sent me a message online that had nothing to do with the death of the physical body. When I finally got around to answering it, something within me felt a strong pull to act now and share a video on sound healing. I had no idea of her impending death but was called to share something spiritual with her. I later learned that the video turned out to be healing therapy for her as she approached her transition.

Another time I was referring to a recipe on my iPhone while cooking dinner at home. A photo I had permission to take for a caregiver of a loved one who was palliative kept popping up on my iPhone. I wondered, why is this photo always popping up? In silence, I looked at the photo and I wondered, are you transitioning now? My hands in prayer position, I bowed with gratitude for all that is, and to the person in the photo, in connection to universal love, I said, "Thank you for all that you are." I later found out the time that the photo appeared on my phone was close to the approximate time when the person in the photo transitioned.

These messages don't come from the thinking mind of thoughts, and when I receive them they don't create anxious feelings or fear of an impending death. These *divine signals* are always present when we are open and receptive to them.

PRISON

I made a conscious choice to be of service. This led me not only to palliative care but to another non-profit organization in service to a correctional centre for incarcerated women.

In a profound inner depth of peace, I felt a calling to connect with inmates. I remembered the moment when health care wasn't there for me during my father's transition, and I wanted to be there for inmates during their suffering. One of the best ways to do this was by way of meditation. I wondered how I could make this happen. I experience a peaceful feeling whenever I merge with others through meditation, where I am grounded in being. I could do the same with fellow human beings in prison.

Whenever I have questions I look to what I've attracted in my life. I ask, what is trying to get my attention? What wants to be seen? Suddenly I thought of a woman I met in a meditation group who had recently mentioned she began facilitating mindfulness meditation at a correctional centre.

In no time, I connected with and joined a couple of women who facilitate a mindfulness and meditation program. The very first time I walked into a prison, I felt very comfortable. I literally felt like I was observing human beings on the set of a movie.

Taking a step back, everything has been created by the human mind of thoughts. To keep it really simple in a complicated world, this means everything we've learned that doesn't serve us can be unlearned. Meditation is a way to calm the nervous system, where we return to stillness, if only for a moment, feeling more at peace within. Inner peace during chaotic times.

In an expansion of awareness, I observed how the roles of inmates and staff unfolded before me in an institutional setting. In my experiences in prison, I've always felt an inner connection to the staff. It's as if there's an invisible agreement between us; whether a meditation facilitator, guard or officer, we are each doing our part in dealing with the consequences of crimes that have been committed.

I continued to observe how in my role as a meditation facilitator, I interacted with the inmates. As we gathered together in a circle, I always made sure to mention that no one is superior or inferior to another, that this is a safe space where everyone is welcome.

Beneath the crimes is our innocence in childhood. Meditation is a portal to the space between our thoughts, between the opposites of right or wrong, good or bad, rich or poor, and between society's expectations of how we should be and how we are. In this gap is innocence, and in this innocence, we exist in each other.

No matter what the women have done, I hold space in the innocence of who we all are, where there is no division of me and you.

When the chatter of the adult mind has a safe space to go deeper within in meditation, even if for a moment or two, each time we open our eyes, there is a sense of calm replacing restlessness.

I believe meditation in prison with inmates, even staff, is the spark that ripples out for the betterment of us all in society. Together, we make a difference to improve the quality of life for humanity.

Part Six:
TRAUMA
AND COLLECTIVE
CONSCIOUSNESS

"As you start to walk on the way, the way appears."

Jalāl al-Dīn Muhammad Rūmī

"Who sees all beings in his own self and his own self in all beings, loses all fear."

The Upanishads

The steps I have taken have all been guided by divine intelligence. Each step I took led me to a new awareness and a new sacred mission. Witnessing human suffering as a child, I was led to selfless service – first to help my father and then to support a wider community of palliative care patients and incarcerated women. And there came a time when I reached another turning point.

After years of feeling comfortable in service, I felt another shift. I found myself restless and "uncomfortable in my comfort zone." I was feeling separate from others more frequently, and I knew something was speaking to me – calling me to make another change.

Ultimately, I came to realize that I needed to go deeper into my own darkness. I needed to do more inner work to deal with the trauma that had been passed down to me from my parents and from generations before them. And I came to see that I should do that difficult work at the level of the collective, with people from different countries and backgrounds who were united by their desire to heal themselves and humanity as a whole. That is what led me to Timeless Wisdom Training. I knew this journey would be painful, but I was still excited. Confronting suffering and pain would lead me to light and deeper truth.

DISCOMFORT BECOMES A CATALYST FOR CHANGE

The compassion and support I was able to provide for patients in palliative care sustained me for many years. I led a beautiful, simple life through sacred action and reached the point where I was comfortable with this very important work. Habits of self-care like daily exercise along with a commitment to be of service became routine.

Then I began to experience uncomfortable feelings of not belonging. Disconnection and loneliness began to slowly rise to the surface, and I found myself increasingly restless for no known reason.

This had been my vision: A being of service, in the role of a palliative care volunteer, where mind and heart come together for the betterment of all. Although I didn't recognize it at the time, the seed to be of service had been planted in me in childhood. I was drawn to authenticity and had dedicated my purpose to being of service. I wanted to connect with everyone, no matter what their role or position and to be part of a supportive team working in unity.

Through many years of service, I had rarely watched the clock. But now, I frequently found myself feeling drained when leaving the hospital. I began feeling left out for the first time, divided from the paid health-care workers operating in the hierarchy. I increasingly identified myself as a lone volunteer in this environment.

I observed "them" from a distance and felt an invisible disconnection. The opposites of "paid" and "unpaid" played out before me in my mind. For a short time, I compared "me and them" and felt an inner longing for human connection, just as I had done at times in childhood. I wondered: "Where do I belong? Why am I even doing this work?"

Staff work to get paid, and rightly so, doing work in a system built from the educated mind of thoughts. There seems to be no time for the heart, which I noticed can be trampled on as being too soft, too emotional, too connecting and too loving in a fear-based conditioned world.

I had no idea where this inner pain and suffering came from. But I knew it was time to go deeper into my own darkness to see what was on the other side. A time for growth.

I have learned to accept and embrace my feelings of suffering as they arise. In doing so, giving myself a universal hug and leaving more space to receive a higher intelligence to guide me further. I was aware that pain and suffering had something to teach me. Asking a question like, "What is trying to get my attention?" leaves me open to receiving answers. These answers take me deeper into loving action.

Walking along a corridor in hospice, I began hearing the words "Global. Go global."

GUIDED TO GO GLOBAL

For a long time, I had wanted to visit Stettin, Germany, now Szczecin, Poland, which had been my mother's home before and during World War II. Just before COVID-19 was declared a pandemic in 2020 by the World Health Organization, I had been booked to go there in June and was very much looking forward to returning to my roots where my family was separated during the war. However, due to all the uncertainty and concerns about protecting my health, I cancelled my flight while also stopping all in-person visits as a palliative care volunteer. There was a higher calling at work and now I had an opportunity to explore my discomfort and chart a new path.

I remained home and deepened my process through meditation and movement through yoga. I received spiritual initiations and new insights, heightening my awareness of mystical knowledge. In silence, I made notes on paper of what was trying to get my attention, capturing words, phrases and feelings. I deepened my contemplation of nature, looking out my window at the trees swaying in the wind, the continuous formation of clouds in the sky, the birds flying by.

I was drawn to unity in this world of separation. I had an inner hunger for human connection where people would come together for the sake of all of humanity. The word "global" arrived. "Global. Global." This calling reverberated in my mind, the intensity driving me to take further action.

Then, I observed my ego quickly sneaking in. "Why would you want to do that? Nobody cares. You don't even like to be seen. You're getting older." I accepted these fearful thoughts before they eventually disappeared, thereby stopping them in their tracks before they developed into an ongoing story in my mind that would not serve me.

I knew I could change such thoughts and adopt a different mindset, one of connection, abundance and possibility, one that was open and receptive to the unknown mystery wanting to emerge through me.

I also had an internal push to answer the call to write a book. I had resisted this call for many years. My thoughts had held me back: "I'm not ready yet. I'll receive a bigger push later, and I'll know when the time is right." I knew that whenever I resisted something, it would persist, and my body would become constricted, rather than expansive and open. Deep down, I knew I could become ill if I didn't answer the call. I knew these divine messages of cosmic intelligence guide the way and they never fail. All I had to do was show up.

The message arrived. "Write. Just write." Just like the signal that arrived to direct me to volunteer in hospice, the signals became more powerful in their insistence of a new direction: I am to write and to go global, now. I finally said, "Yes! I am willing."

Silence, an ancient inner voice, a knowing of the unknown, a deep eternal longing to be expressed was rising to the surface. An inner responsibility to be seen, to be heard, to be felt, globally, was emerging that was not coming from the conditioned, limited self. I knew I had to go deep, very deep, to deepen my process. This calling was so much bigger than me.

Why do I have an inner calling to go global? I knew I could no longer do this work alone. I had an inner thirst to work through the culturally imposed limitation of a divisive world that would no longer keep me silent, where mystical knowledge speaks.

I knew I needed to connect with others on a global scale to accelerate an inner urgency to help humanity evolve – to expand consciousness. I wanted to come together in oneness with others who are open to mystical wisdom for the greater good.

I knew I needed to break the silence: the silence of unspeakable trauma of World War II in Mother, the unspoken silence of disease in Father, where both have been the very foundation of my path. My assignment, my unique purpose, continues.

I am open and receptive to what wants to emerge through this human vessel. It feels both huge and frightening. In service to humanity, like a lotus flower blossoms, I am called to go global to express what comes through. A responsibility, a commitment, to the next chapter.

CHAOS TO CALM TO ACTION

Today, humanity appears to be even more out of balance, with many of us disconnected from our bodies, from one another and from Mother Earth. We struggle with a desperate need to be seen, to be heard, to be the best, to be right in a highly competitive world. No matter what accolades we receive from society, many of us are experiencing anxiety, depression, greed and rage.

It's as if we've been simmering in this disconnection of sizing one another up in the material world for many years, and now we're at the boiling point. I wonder, "Is more disease on the horizon?" Mental health problems are definitely on the rise, and for good reason. War continues to this day and our disconnection from the planet has led to unprecedented threats from climate change.

I think many of us can agree we are not going through all of this pain and suffering for nothing. Individual, collective and intergenerational trauma has happened and is still happening, and within it, there is a treasure, gems to guide humanity through our suffering.

My inner search for global connection led to my discovery of the first global Timeless Wisdom Training offered in the United States and Germany, simultaneously. For the first time, I learned about Thomas Hübl and his story, which sparked a connection in me. His grandfather had served as a soldier for the German Third Reich. As a young boy he listened to his Opa share stories of WWII. I felt strongly that this forum was the answer to many of my insistent questions.

Collective trauma healing would be empowered by online sessions between both hubs, and for in-person meetings, I chose northern Germany, not too far from my mother's birthplace. Here was my opportunity to make the trip to Stettin that had been cancelled during the pandemic and to come together with people from around the world on a healing journey.

AT LONG LAST, A VISIT TO STETTIN

I have my train ticket in hand, and I can't believe I'm finally going to Stettin.

I'm so excited!!

I love travelling, especially to explore new cultures in countries I'd never been to. However, my first visit to Poland would be a different kind of trip. It was part of my search for healing in the face of trauma.

More than 77 years had passed since 1945, and yet, those long-ago events lived within me. I was a Canadian descendent of a German war survivor with intergenerational trauma embedded in the fabric of my being. What emotions would this visit evoke in me and how would I process the experience? I had come here to connect with my mother's life and discover more about myself and the wounds I carried from my ancestors.

My daughter, pregnant at the time, accompanied me on this journey. We were travelling from Berlin and were scheduled to change trains in a small town in Poland called Rzepin (Reppen, Germany, before the war). Then we would carry on to Szczecin, renamed from Stettin with the post-war changes in the boundaries of Germany and Poland.

Seated on the train, I allowed myself to search for connections with Mother in this land that she had once been a part of. I actually knew very little. Did my displaced mother travel this route when forced to leave Stettin and head to southern Germany? How many times did she make this trip in happier times before the war to visit with family and friends? I didn't know the answers, but the very act of asking the questions helped me feel her spirit.

We arrived in Rzepin, and I stepped off the train onto Polish soil for the first time. As my daughter went ahead to check where we would board the next train, I stood near the tracks with our small bags of luggage. In these initial moments, I felt somewhat trancelike, and I was aware that I had "tunnel vision." I wasn't as open and receptive to everything as I normally would have been in a new country.

As I began slowly walking in the direction my daughter had taken, I found myself keeping my eyes on the ground. I was not ready to make any human connection in the land of my mother's birth. With a brief glance upwards, I noticed signs written in Polish and heard the Polish language spoken by a few people nearby. This is Poland now; my mother's birthright as a German citizen has dissolved. I became aware of anger entering my mind and thought, "This is not Poland. This is Germany!" Take it slow, I tell myself.

I met up with my daughter, and together we walked to the scheduled platform to wait for our train to Stettin. I broke out of my narrow trancelike state and opened myself up. In my childhood, Mother had expressed joy on a few occasions about her life in Stettin, and I wanted to feel what she may have felt during those times. I was torn between these happy moments and the darkness underneath it, the suffering borne out of war.

Standing outside on the platform, we felt the heat, and so we took off our jackets and the masks we had worn on the train. It felt so good and healthy to feel the warm sunshine on our skin. Nearby was an older gentleman standing with a young couple who often looked in our direction, appearing to know we were foreigners. The older man walked over to us, and with a smile and speaking in broken English, he told us he was from Rzepin. He was there with his daughter and her partner to see them off as they returned home after visiting him. They would also be on the train to Stettin and would continue on from there.

The young couple walked towards us. We all introduced ourselves and shared our experiences. In this interchange, I had forgotten all about why I was here as we connected through conversation and laughter.

Then an announcement in Polish came over the loudspeaker. My daughter and I didn't understand a word, but our kind new friends let us know the news: the train was delayed by one hour. The young man told us he would help us along the way, and so he did. Once the train did arrive, the couple found their way to a compartment car with three seats facing another three seats. Once they settled in, they didn't hesitate to invite us to join them. The young man helped with our bags as we all exchanged smiles before settling into our seats to continue with the journey towards our destinations.

The blinds on the windows of the train were almost entirely closed. I closed my eyes to rest. In fact, at that point, I didn't want to look out through the window so I could avoid my dark vision of fellow human beings fleeing on foot and fighting for their very survival in the woods. For now, the interior of the train was my cocoon, my protection from the horrors of war. There would be time later in the trip for me to honour the suffering of my mother with a direct gaze.

Human connection had brought moments of joy for us already on our journey, through the kindness of the young couple. Sitting still on the train, I remembered we had some Canadian maple syrup tapped in Northwestern Ontario in glass bottles in the shape of a maple leaf. I opened the zipper of my suitcase and with my hand I dug deep into my bag, finally bringing one bottle to the surface. I handed it over to the couple in acceptance and appreciation for their generosity. They received this simple gift with beautiful smiles and a welcoming nod of thanks.

The next stop was where we would all get off the train. The young couple continued to guide and direct us before we thanked them once again and all parted in different directions.

When we stepped off the train, I once again found the environment heavy and numbing. All signs were in Polish and we were surrounded by Polish-speaking people who all seemed to know where to go. It didn't take us long to find our way out of the train station. It would take approximately 30 minutes to walk to our Airbnb apartment.

As I pulled my luggage over the cobblestones, I was getting hot, tired and thirsty. "This is nothing to complain about," I thought. "Mother and other family members had survived war right here in this city." Becoming increasingly uncomfortable, I stopped and took off my jacket before continuing on. I paused with the sun shining over me, and I welcomed feelings of gratitude for being here. Nearby was a small, fenced area where some children were kicking around a ball, reminding me of the human capacity for joy in the moment.

When we arrived at our apartment, we found it to be spacious and beautiful. I offered to sleep on the comfortable mattress on the floor in the living room and to give my pregnant daughter the bedroom, with its large bed.

It was slowly getting darker outside. We decided to stretch our legs and walked to a nearby restaurant, a small and cosy place that served Ukrainian food. Just over an eight-hour drive was the Ukrainian border, where the Russia-Ukraine war was still happening. Imagine after all these years, war still continues. Have we not learned anything?

At a nearby grocery store, I bought purple grapes, a large white candle and red carnations, which I put in a vase and placed on a small round table in our apartment. I took a 5 X 7 black and white photo out of an envelope I had put in my travel bag. The photo was of my mother surrounded by my grandparents and many family members before the war. I found some comfort in the thought of my family returning back to Stettin with us, even if it was in the form of a photograph, very likely taken in this city. Every night for the duration of our visit, I lit the candle in homage to my ancestors, then blew it out before we left to venture out for the day.

In the following days, we tried Ukrainian dishes like borsch soup, herring under a blanket, and galushky in mushroom sauce, along with a bottle of lvivske 1715 Ukraine beer. Tasty Polish dishes included spicy cod soup, classic Polish sour soup on organic sourdough served with fried egg, and a classic fish spread from Szczecin, along with a salad with baked beetroot and goose, nuts, goat cheese and honey-mustard sauce. These delicious Polish and Ukrainian dishes – homemade food served straight from the kitchen in a homelike environment – gave us a warm, cosy feeling of togetherness.

We didn't know any Polish nor did we even know how to attempt to pronounce the words. When we spoke English only, we felt the Poles were distant and cold towards us. However, we quickly learned that we could break down barriers by simply attempting to speak their language, even if it was using just one word like "dziękuję ci,"(pronounced jen-koo-yea), meaning "thank you." This was enough to bring about smiles and a sense of connection. This is healing.

We had two addresses to explore where my mother had once lived. Near each one was a park. I soon learned these parks hadn't been too badly damaged by bombing and their beauty endured for people to enjoy today. I welcomed these opportunities to deeply connect with nature, as in my childhood, a strong gateway to inner wisdom.

First, we walked in the large park where huge orange-yellow autumn leaves had fallen to the ground. Most were from towering Platanus x acerifolia trees, commonly known as London plane trees. My senses lit up as we walked through the spectacular scenery before us and took in the sights and smells of the natural world. The maple-leaf-shaped leaves were everywhere and so beautiful.

While experiencing the grandeur of these humongous trees, a young Polish woman walked towards me and gave me a headpiece she had just made using the wax-coloured leaves. Accepting this in awe, I wondered, did the woman know why I was here? I placed it on my head and my daughter took a few photos. When I then attempted to return the headpiece, the smiling woman shook her head, no. Then with the fingers of her two hands she touched her lips before blowing us a kiss. The experience was so magical. A spark was ignited amongst the autumn leaves of these unique trees, our connection to nature, amplified by human interaction.

Then we went to the second park near the home where my mother lived as a child in the 1920s. Here, I found a plaque that said, "The Rose Garden was opened in Szczecin in 1928. 8,000 rosebushes representing different varieties of roses were planted and their number was systematically increased. A lot of old trees and bushes have survived since World War II." For a moment, I thought about the fact that in 1928, it was Stettin,

Germany, and not Szczecin, Poland. I thought of Mother as a young child also connecting to nature in the Rose Garden. It was another experience that allowed my mind to connect to my heart. We are nature. Nature has no boundaries.

As we explored the city, we visited many landmarks that evoked thoughts of my mother. The one that stood out for me was Waly Chrobrego Promenade (known in the German era as Hakenter-rasse), a walkway that offered spectacular views as it traced the Oder River. This man-made structure was designed and con-structed between 1902 and 1921 and had remarkably survived the ravages of war. Again, images of my mother came to me. I thought of her walking this promenade many times throughout her young life while living in the beautiful city of Stettin.

I searched everywhere for something I could purchase with the name "Stettin" on it, but I found nothing. Perhaps this search was my way to validate the narrative still playing in my mind of my mother's life prior to war.

We also visited the Szczecin Underground Routes, a museum located under the train station. It was here where I finally found the word "Stettin" written. Built in 1941 during World War II, this German bunker could hold as many as 5,000 civilians during air raids. I imagined the sound of sirens and how frightening it would be to hear the noise of planes flying overhead.

The bunker felt dark, divided, cold and organized. Walking through the tunnels, I experienced moments where I felt numb and other moments where I felt curious. There were mannequins with bright, turquoise-coloured eyes, representing Germans: male mannequins standing upright on one side and females on the opposite side of a narrow tunnel. They were all dressed in beautiful fashionable clothing. We saw a small square area at one time used for women (including pregnant women) and children, depicted by more mannequins, this time with gas masks on their faces. An information plaque in the tunnel says, "The walls are covered with phosphor paint. When it is dark, the paint lights the room for about 30 minutes. This paint is often lifesaving because people can see how to move in the shelter."

I noticed the words *"Ruhe bewahren,"* meaning "Stay calm." I don't know if Mother had ever entered this main bunker; there were many shelters throughout the city. But I'm sure she had heard the words "stay calm" many times during the war, and I wondered whether that message had something to do with her calm presence during my father's gastrointestinal bleed all those years later – a beautiful gift to guide us through suffering.

I thought about the silence of my mother and how millions of people remain in silence for the rest of their lives, never speaking of war. During times of war, the admonition to stay silent is often the key to survival, but the silence that may follow for years afterwards can be toxic to the body, causing disease, and in that way, becoming a threat to survival. It's been said the wounds of our fathers and ancestors are transmitted for three to four generations when trauma is not metabolized. I calmed myself and thought about how the intelligence coming through each one of us during the dark night of the soul, our pain and suffering, is an inner resource. A calm, divine presence remains no matter what is happening in and around us – even inner peace in what can be a chaotic world.

The day we were to depart the city was All Saint's Day, a public holiday when people gather with candles and visit the graves of their loved ones. In the beauty of early morning silence, I watched the flame of the candle flicker. Then I looked at The family photo, which included Mother and Oma.

Through reflection, I felt the life of women on Mother Earth, in particular, the natural divine feminine energy of love and compassion. Had the controlling and violent wounded *masculine*, filled with anger and hate, overshadowed the *feminine*, the suppressed voice of the feminine still living with a victim mentality of self-shame? Humanity is still caught up in this division today. Both men and women have access to divine feminine and masculine energy. Once we know this, we can welcome the complete and healthy versions of both; we no longer have to live this old, conditioned life of disconnection and lack of freedom.

I thought of the time when my mother was forced to leave her city and leave her mother's body behind. Tears started streaming down my cheeks. Oma's body was left here, and now we would leave too. I was reminded of a deeper knowing: We are not the body, and just like Mother, like Father, Oma is nowhere and everywhere.

Leaving Stettin, I had a lot to digest and integrate. I hadn't really connected with Stettin as much as I would have liked. I never felt like celebrating the moments I saw in those old black-and-white photographs of my mother, a time when everyone was happy and alive before war broke out. And yet, I felt connected in emptiness. Pulling our luggage over the cobblestones, my daughter and I walked back towards the main train station to return to Germany.

Standing in the train station, I feel the Underground Routes beneath my feet, once again reminded that everything has been created by the mind through divisive action over centuries. I thought about the next phase of my journey, where I would participate in the Timeless Wisdom Training sessions.

I had just touched the surface of the underlying layers of humanity's darkness. I knew I would somehow have to do my part on a global scale to break this cycle, connecting with other people who are open to divine intelligence to guide us through human suffering – where inner peace is waiting to be discovered within each one of us, where there is freedom for generations to come.

I stepped back outside for a moment to look out at the Oder River to connect with water, the symbol of fertility and purity, an invaluable life-sustaining force. I looked towards the entrance of the museum beside me, and I thought of fellow human beings running in fear into the underground shelter. I felt saddened by a thick overlying shadow of darkness. I felt some connection to this city that will always be Stettin for me.

In this world, separation continues to limit us, adding another layer of horrific pain and suffering. And beneath these layers is humanity's connection to Mother Earth.

GERMANY IN-PERSON

When we arrived back in Germany, my daughter and I parted ways, and I headed to the in-person retreat. I had a lot of experiences in Stettin to digest and integrate before immersing myself in more trauma healing. There was a part of me that felt I could have used a couple of more days to process. I wasn't so eager to go deeper into collective trauma healing just yet – but I did.

Once I arrived at the next location, I recognized that I felt slightly off. I wasn't fully centred, but I embraced my fragility and opened myself up to curiosity, and to the joyfulness that could arise from this new experience.

I soon found myself feeling connected to this global group. I sensed that everyone there felt as I did – that we were done with the conditioned identity of division often reflected through greed and violence in the world. From all walks of life, we answered a calling to come together for a higher purpose – to heal collective trauma. Everyone made a commitment to take full responsibility to do this work to heal the inner wound and thus, contribute to the healing of the whole.

A trauma retreat is a place where people can express themselves without fear of judgement from others. There is to be no debate, no "cross-talking," similar to the norms practised in group therapy.

In this safe container of sharing, the group remained in silent presence while anyone shared their vulnerabilities. Regardless of how we identified ourselves by gender, position, title, accolades, country, language or skin colour, we recognized these external categories were irrelevant to who we are at the core.

A true sense of belonging creates a vessel for collective healing and transformation to occur in a divisive world.

One participant stood up and told the group that being in Germany was difficult because they felt emotional pain simply listening to the sound of the German language. Everyone sat in a depth of silence as they contemplated what had just been shared.

This comment hit me hard. It instantly touched part of a frozen layer in my physical body and triggered something deep within me that I had no words for. This group was made up of people from many different countries, and it included the descendants of Jews (and others) who had been through the horrors of the Holocaust and the descendants of Germans who had remained in Germany after the war. All of us were seeking the opportunity to heal our individual and collective wounds.

"Listening to the sound of the German language" continued to echo in my mind. I felt my body become tense and constricted and sensed tears building up behind my eyes, but I managed to hold them in.

Shortly after this sharing it was time to take a break for dinner, and so we walked next door into the dark night towards another building to eat. I became more aware that I was holding my breath in and finding it difficult to exhale. I told myself I needed to push back what wanted to express itself, at least for now.

Images flashed before me: Hitler, soldiers, the sound of German voices on black and white war documentaries, then the Nazi salute. I remembered my mother's words steeped in shame and pain. "*Wir mussten unsere Hand heben.* We had to raise our hand. *Mussten.* We had to."

I couldn't yet bring myself to walk inside the building for dinner, and so I sat alone in the dark on a large outdoor swing near the entranceway. Maybe I could distract myself a bit before entering the dining room to eat with everyone; maybe swinging would help soothe me? Resisting the feelings within my body, I continued to think about my dilemma. What if someone sees me and decides to walk towards me? I feared I would burst into uncontrollable tears.

This was about my body cracking into a layer of very old intergenerational trauma. I needed to honour this intelligence, and it was telling me I had to find a private space where I could release my tears and go deeper into my inner wounds.

If I walked away from dinner, I'd miss a delicious vegetarian meal and the evening talk afterward (a favourite of mine). But I realized that being alone was the best decision for me at this moment. I also knew I had many fellow human beings around me who would be available to see, hear and feel me, when I would need them. As I abruptly left the swing, I met others walking towards me who were still on their way to dinner. I didn't make eye contact.

I was finally alone in the dark night, away from everyone. I walked on the bike path alongside a country road and found myself remembering the dirt path that ran along the highway in Wabigoon, where in childhood, we had watched out for a lone wolf. Like a waterfall, I could feel tears pouring out of my left eye only. It wasn't long before both eyes were filled and tears began streaming down my cheeks.

I returned to my childhood. "Mommy, I'm here in Germany." I looked out into the beautiful dark country surrounding me while feeling the fresh air on my skin, asking, "Did bombs fall here too? Were adults and children fleeing in the darkness – right here? Was everyone running and hiding, trying to survive the brutalities of war?"

Wir mussten unsere Hand heben. We had to raise our hand. *Mussten.* We had to. The sound of the German language. I could feel more tears streaming down my cheeks.

And then something shifted within me.

I became aware of the clean breeze on my face in the dark night. The air was so fresh to breathe in. I looked up to the sky and noticed the full moon shining brightly. I also saw the planet Venus and a star near the moon and then perceived an invisible shape of a triangle, connecting them all. I was fearless in the night, even now in this place of vulnerability, and I could feel a bond with humanity, worldwide. Something had cracked open, and I felt calm and centred.

I continued walking, and when I was back in my room, I went straight to bed and cried some more, releasing tears that needed to be released.

When I returned to the group early the next morning, I noticed the shapes of triangles everywhere along the way. I was reminded of the Sri Yantra, a mystical diagram including circles, triangles and an eight-petal lotus, which I have often meditated on. The central triangle, the Bindu, represents pure consciousness, a sure sign of an entry point to our spiritual essence.

Something more wanted to rise to the surface and express itself, but I didn't know what it was. I wasn't certain that I could share my previous night's experience with the others. Looking back, I recognize that I didn't want anyone to tell me I wasn't feeling what I was feeling. If so, the old conditioning could easily shut me up, again. The old way of protecting myself by withdrawing was in the way. But this was not a space for feedback unless asked; it was a space for healing and honouring the wisdom coming through.

I felt raw and vulnerable. I was sensitive to every comment that others shared, and I could envision myself on my knees, uncontrollably releasing it all in front of everyone. What do I do with this rising fear of exposing the conditioned me?

During a short break, before returning to the group, I found my way to the participant who expressed how she felt when listening to the sound of the German language. I gave her a hug and thanked her for sharing, mentioning it had awakened something so raw, deep within me.

Still feeling vulnerable, my mind returned to anxious thoughts of the future. I realized that I needed to speak with someone in private to prepare myself for what could rise up in me. So, I shared one-on-one with a psychotherapist and the experience was truly healing.

I felt such comfort in having a calm fellow human being hold space for me to speak about whatever needed to be expressed. I had no idea what I would speak about, but I knew I needed to release these words for another to witness. I realized that although I had done the same for many people on my path of service, there was not always someone available who could do it for me.

Imagine creating a safe container where we openly share and witness each other, as we express what is happening within us in the moment. Honouring the underlying intelligence in somatic feelings like fatigue, joint or muscle pain, headache, and dizziness arising due to old trauma, openly sharing experiences of mysticism, so that we can learn and grow together.

In more ways than we know, we are all connected through the traumatization of the world. I believe it's time to acknowledge and accept trauma, as well as mysticism.

I spoke about the ancestral trauma my mother passed onto me that I buried for so long. I spoke of human suffering witnessed during Father's bleeding crises, the silence of war, the needless suffering of humanity and about human separation in a conditioned society. I spoke about mysticism and cosmic intelligence and about divine purpose. I spoke of the calling I received to go global, leading me here to this group.

After this sharing, I no longer felt constricted and became more open and receptive, and much lighter. This is healing. However, I didn't want to become too comfortable after this sharing because I knew I had to go deeper to feel my way through more layers. I felt an inner responsibility to embrace what my ancestors couldn't, to make my contribution to break the trauma cycle from rippling out to future generations.

Although it can be difficult to express, I love trauma healing. Why would I even say that? I love it because I know trauma is not who I am, nor does it define me (or us). Allowing myself to voice and release the pain in a safe space as it arises is a pathway to the deepest truth.

An image comes to my mind when I consider the effort of healing collective trauma. An image of hard-packed soil – dense, difficult to penetrate and inhospitable to life – where organisms cannot easily survive. This hard soil represents unexpressed layers of trauma passed on from generation to generation. On a larger scale, the hard soil represents the silent underlying collective trauma that has been buried, frozen in time, which can show up when it rises to the surface through anger, hurt, blame, complaining and gossip, and hate and division.

Our task as we move toward healing is to turn this into rich, organic soil, which allows water and air to move more easily in and around plants' roots, resulting in healthier plants.

As I share with other humans and someone shares back, it's like using a spoon and feeding one another nourishment for the soul within a sacred space of deep listening, in presence, and an undigested layer is cracked open. Bit by bit, it is slowly digested and integrated, and healing occurs.

Each time a little bit of hard soil is removed, I feel lighter, and a space opens up and allows me to breathe a little deeper and exhale a little longer. When stuck energy is cleared, I join the water of the river of my soul where the very breath I breathe, breathes me. In doing so, the hard soil slowly changes into a richer soil.

When I speak in loving action through my individual sharing, I touch the surface of the hard soil, and merge with the unspoken that wants to be seen, I dig a little deeper. In that space, I am able to receive the light each person shares with me.

In giving, I empty what is full. In receiving, I fill what is empty. By acting in collective connection, we can create the rich organic soil that nurtures life and healing for all.

Without any expectations of anything, the wisdom of self-knowledge rises.

I had just scratched the surface of expressing collective trauma through this body temple. This time, rather than swallowing and suppressing the effects of trauma, I used my quiet, silent voice to share with a worldwide community on a global scale.

GLOBAL COMMUNITY ON-LINE

There is beauty in trauma healing. Especially when the voice is witnessed, when bodily sensations and physical responses are welcome, where mysticism shows up and all is happening within a safe space.

Is it difficult? Absolutely.

Is it worth it? Absolutely.

I am committed to do my part to break through this old, conditioned cycle of human division. My pain and suffering is not who I am. Open to the expression of what wants to reveal itself, I receive guidance and lessons while my wounds heal.

I sat on two yoga blocks and a small cushion in front of my laptop during one of our first online sessions. I was part of a triad with two Jewish women. We were randomly selected from more than 400 online participants. After we each briefly introduced ourselves, I instantly felt the warmth and comfort in our group of three. Then we sat silently in presence with each other and closed our eyes.

For me, the warm feeling slowly changed to a cool, light breeze that was very alive. I was aware of my mind beginning to identify me as the daughter of a German WWII survivor.

I began to panic as my mind quickly jumped to the fear of the unknown, a dark time in human history. Something during World War II wanted to express itself through me. Suddenly, I felt the urge to take flight and leave this session. I quickly opened my eyes and abruptly stopped those feelings, freezing for a moment before connecting in presence with these beautiful women.

In silence, I thought, "Something frightening wants to reveal itself." I was aware of this fear approaching, but I embraced and welcomed it. Before leaving our triad we each had an opportunity to share what we experienced – without any feedback (unless we requested it). Through sharing, we learned each one of us had been affected by collective trauma in various ways.

Inner work can be frightening when painful thoughts of past conditioning re-emerge. It's easy to get sucked back into a story of human suffering. The more aware we are, the more we become the watcher, the observer of the human story, until we are no longer caught up in the tale of suffering.

I am reminded that I am not my thoughts; I am the observer of my thoughts. Every time we become aware of painful thoughts or of ego-driven actions, we not only stop them in their tracks, but our awareness also becomes more expansive. We let go of division and are guided towards human connection, and our thoughts and words come from Universal Love.

I felt really excited to be connecting with an international online group. I felt energized, with an increased need to move my body. And so, before the next scheduled online meeting, I danced freely around the house to a backdrop of lively music, which took me out of my mind of thoughts. I remained in presence to the dance of the universe.

Once online, I listened with my whole body as participants shared their feelings and thoughts. As I released tension and energy stored in my body, I experienced physical responses. I began to notice a light headache, then a bit of nausea, pain on the lower right side of my back and some restlessness. Rather than trying to analyze it, I continued to embrace and honour everything as it showed up.

Intellectually, I don't know exactly what it is, but something within me resonates with what is being shared. I'm aware of my neck getting tight and then my entire body becomes stiff and constricted. The sadness is growing in me, and I feel the pressure of tears seeking release. Going deeper into this process, I sit with my grief. The unconscious is becoming conscious of itself, as I immerse myself in the feelings, further integrating what has been undigested for far too long.

As a mirror to what others share, we strengthen our interdependence. In this work, I need you for support as much as you need me. This is not about becoming needy; it's about supporting each other by way of presence. As we merge together in healing, we rise together in universal love, taking loving action through service.

As we continued to share with each other, I experienced more physical pain and more strong emotions, eventually allowing tears to flow out. Releasing tears gives me a little more spaciousness to receive, and therefore, I am more open to give. In this dynamic of giving and receiving is an exchange of energy that is no longer stagnant.

There were moments when I stepped away from the screen and lay down in the foetal position. It felt so heavy and yet I was open to whatever wanted to move through me and out. Deep down I know I'm going back thousands of years into an unconscious story still played out today.

Healing this old story of division begins with me.

No matter how good our intentions may be, when the ego sneaks in and rises to the surface in places like education, religion, spirituality, health care, government and other facets of human life, it does none of us any good. But what happens when we set an intention while bringing our attention to it as it unfolds?

I had an opportunity to explore this concept in another online triad. We each agreed to set an *intention* and to bring *attention* to what was happening inside ourselves. Then, we would describe our process as it happened, to invite a deeper connection.

In a safe environment with like-hearted people, I offered to go first. I hadn't fully landed in this space yet, and as I closed my eyes, I slowly grounded myself in connection with breath.

I was smiling as I voiced my intention to bring in divine intelligence. Until now, I had only done this alone, and it was the very first time this intention was being witnessed.

Open to receive, I sat in silence. I envisioned the energy of this intelligence moving from the top of my head down to the base of my spine, and back up and out of my body. I begin to describe my inner world to the others as it unfolded.

I travelled down to the bottom of my spine and back up, when I noticed I only went as far as the area of my head where I felt my brain to be. There was some stagnation interrupting the flow of energy, and I knew the path was not yet entirely clear. I noticed my inner voice was slightly conflicted.

I put my attention in the area of my brain, and I feel resistance beginning to dissipate and more space opening up. My attention continues to move upward above my head. With this movement, my spinal cord and brain, the top of my head and up are open to receive the natural flow. I settle deeper into my whole body.

And then it happened. It was as if someone took a ball of light and dropped it into my body from the top of my head. Expanding and rippling out, the glowing ball of light (about the size of a billiard ball) moves down to the bottom of my spine. Then it moves back up to the middle of my chest where it continued to flow out to all. Tears of pure joy streamed down my face.

Later, when each of the triads came together with a larger group to discuss all of our experiences, I was interested to learn that one of the participants in another triad had also felt a ball of light happening within him.

In my triad, it was my turn to witness the words of the other participants as they described their own intention and inner process.

What I noticed was whenever someone shared their feelings of shame, I instantly dropped into the energy body located at the base of my spine. This area's function is safety, groundedness and survival. The ball of light remained in the area of my heart where its function is empathy, compassion and peace. The heart serves as our centre for love for oneself and others, while the top of the head represents the divine energy of universal consciousness and life's purpose.

I was grounded with empathy, love and compassion for the pain and suffering (shame) of a fellow human being, while being open to divine intelligence (the ball of light in my heart).

These experiences solidified for me the truth of what I had been living as an individual. Now I had connected with an international group also open to this intelligence that I long felt was my guide.

I no longer had to do this alone.

To be witnessed globally in the present moment as I expressed what had been suppressed within me for so long was true freedom. I was aware that I naturally smiled each time we returned to the larger group from doing our triad work.

Looking back, this whole experience of writing and trauma healing, feels as though I've walked barefoot in the nude, fearless, through a dark wild jungle.

We exist in each other. Feel that for a moment. The mind has separated us for far too long. The more I commit to this work as an individual and the more we do this together, I know that we can change humanity's course for the betterment of us all.

INDIVIDUAL TO COLLECTIVE IMPACT ON THE WORLD – NO LONGER ALONE

Many of us have become more aware that the human race and planet Earth are undergoing an unprecedented transition.

This can be an exciting time if we would just take a step back and get out of the unconscious, conditioned story of the past. The old is collapsing as a new beginning is emerging. In between the old and new is pain and suffering. Within human suffering is the inner spark of light that we are.

It's time to awaken to a deeper reality of who we are and what we are here to do by way of conscious service on the planet. Within these challenging and exciting times is something so profound that wants to reveal itself.

Trauma likes to separate and blaming someone else feeds into this separation. In our relationships, this may include parents, partners, co-workers or anyone out there we may fall victim to. As soon as they trigger us, we may come down hard on them, even harder on ourselves. If we take a step back, our parents and those before them have been born into unresolved trauma too. Yes, they may have done us wrong, but when does it end?

We must take responsibility for the trauma that lives within us. Often we use our trauma as an excuse to follow a path of self-destruction, hurting ourselves and others along the way. It's time to take responsibility to move towards ending this painful cycle.

In this trauma work, there are moments when I feel sadness, fatigue and irritability. Trauma work can be heavy. I've experienced confusion, restlessness, repetition, and numbness. I have become stiff as if frozen. There were moments when it was difficult to untangle myself from the old repetitive story. In awareness, I was able to not only embrace and accept it all, I was able to remove myself from the story in order to heal and transform the old into a new way of being. A conscious choice to go into deeper layers that are frozen is my responsibility to myself, my family and ancestors in an attempt to break this cycle.

Sometimes I want to be alone in this heaviness to process and digest this experience. In other moments, I feel an inner sense of restlessness and curiosity where I feel a need to move my body through stretching, walking or dance. Then there are moments of calm and contentment when I sit in reflection.

This healing work can be exhausting, and yet it must be honoured and respected for its intelligence. I am slowly moving through painful feelings and emotions of undigested trauma in all of us. Feeling and expressing these emotions as they arise while in the presence of others isn't always easy. The more I bring attention to them, hold and hug them as they move through me, it gets better. In doing this trauma healing, I can feel an inner shift happening. There is growth; even though I don't know exactly what that looks like, I can feel it.

As I have shared, there have been moments in my life when I feel like I'm doing this work, and having these spiritual experiences, alone. In answer to the call, a transformation has now taken place. I've merged with a global group of like-hearted fellow human beings, who are also open to divine intelligence. I no longer feel like I'm doing this work alone, and this gives me hope for the human race and our planet.

There's no turning back. Trauma healing continues to call to me.

Wherever you are, whatever you're doing, no matter what your life has been like – listen, for you too may be called to heal. As I see it, when each individual is receptive to divine intelligence, we are guided to be of service for the highest good of all. Here lies our assignment, our unique soul's purpose, which lives through us.

You can nurture presence and call upon your higher intelligence on your own or with others. Remember to respect this intelligence and trust it; let go of the scepticism that many express about mystical knowledge.

For me, I was guided in presence on my own, and then over time, to smaller and then larger groups.

Now I am experiencing the power of joining with a global community. In witnessing presence, we've created a safe container where we openly share with each other. In this global sharing, our human similarities bring us closer together.

I feel seen.
I feel heard.
I feel I belong.

A transition from individual to collective slowly begins to transpire, as collective suffering merges into a calm presence. Creating more spaciousness, individual presence merges with group presence. We now come from a collective group presence open to divine presence.

We each go deeper within, together moving into higher vibrational frequencies, evolving into higher states of collective consciousness. We share the same intention of contributing to healing collective trauma. We are committed, motivated and devoted.

In this shared intention, we share the same vision of healing trauma. As we heal our own trauma, it ripples out to heal collective trauma. Further rippling out into healing relationships in our workplace, into areas like education, health care, government and to our lives, with ourselves and our families, and then onto global issues facing humanity like world hunger, poverty, global health, the climate crisis and war.

It's a difficult and an exciting time.

As we evolve into higher states of consciousness, and the individual merges with the collective, we all return to wholeness. We return to inner peace, love and joy. We come from empathy, love and compassion for each other. We are guided and motivated to take action as we move through what can be misery in a divisive world. From here we continue moving through pain and suffering with more people, lifting us up as we rise together.

Rising together in unity consciousness, we are interconnected in harmony. In this group coherence, we share the same intention, the same vision. Each soul's purpose becomes one Soul purpose, where Life's purpose lives us. Here we move into sacred conscious action, each one of us a unique expression of the unified whole guided by divine intelligence. Together we accelerate the process, as more and more of us come together with the same intention and the same vision.

Life's purpose lives through the collective, accelerating our work through acts of service for the betterment of the human race and Mother Earth.

Imagine the impact of shifting this repetitive cycle from trauma to returning to inner peace, love and joy for all, for generations to come.

RETURN TO PRESENCE

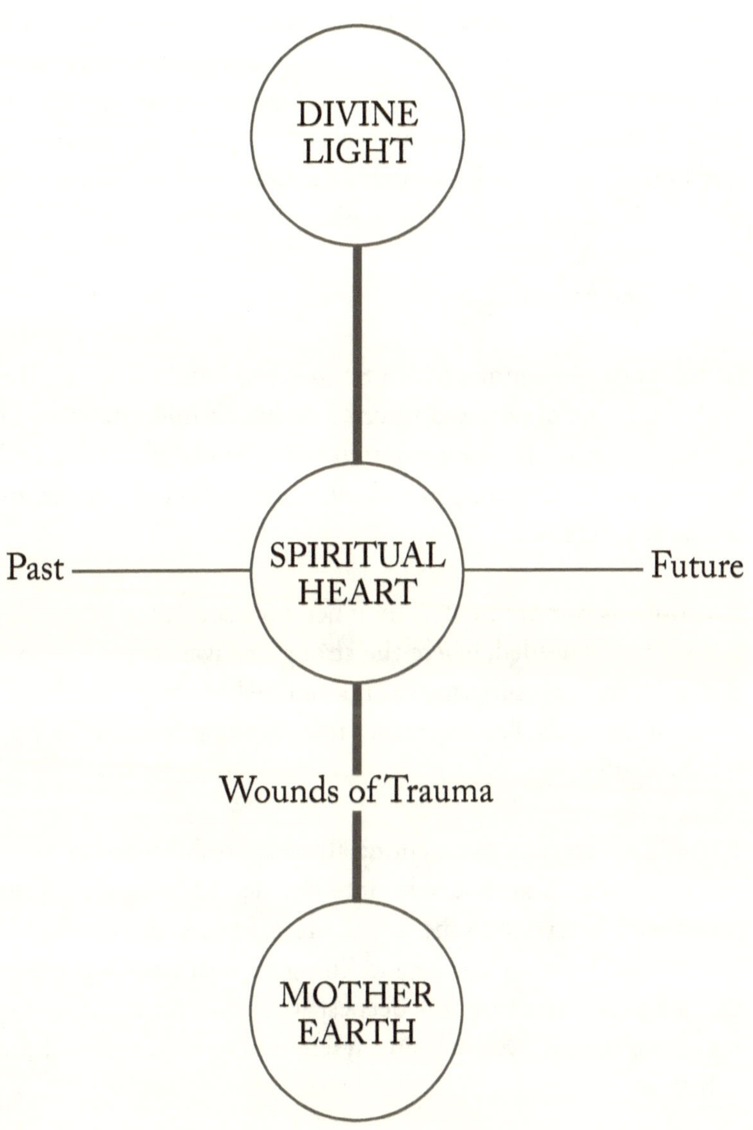

Break the Trauma Cycle
Rise from Deepest Wound

When we draw upon the intelligence of Mother Earth, our Spiritual Heart and the Light of Divine Intelligence, we return to presence, Pure Consciousness. The light we surrender to and are open to receive seeps through our deepest wounds of trauma, past and future dissolve and intelligence comes through to guide. Through a state of presence, we arrive at inner peace and freedom where we take conscious action from the True Self, even in the midst of a chaotic world.

Vertical line/horizontal line

In this vertical alignment with Source, spaciousness opens. The horizontal line of past and future dissolve, an understanding of pure intelligence is rising through the wounds of trauma, and there's a joyful participation and celebration of life through conscious action for all.

A conscious commitment to do inner work and/or to be of selfless service is needed, where the strong are available to support the weak through suffering (as needed), which may change between individuals. Feeling, rather than running from, is the way through suffering.

There is an urgency to accepting the responsibility to do inner work in order to grow deeper into the depths of healing. Our inner work is service to the world. Here, I break the vicious cycle of trauma for my family and lineage. I heal what my ancestors couldn't. I rise from my deepest wound, while breaking the repetitive trauma cycle within myself, family, ancestors and the collective.

As we are well aware, hate and war are still happening, and suffering has happened and is happening, as in the Israel-Hamas war. With a return to presence, I heal past trauma every time I integrate my wounds, planting seeds of healing that germinate in the future, rippling out to others. A state of inner spaciousness during spiritual practices, service, even my deepest healing in trauma, presence is always available.

Embodiment of this divine intelligence is our inner guide to put grace into action.

APPENDIX

INSIGHTS ON ACCESSING YOUR HIGHER INTELLIGENCE

We can all find the path to accessing our higher intelligence, our True Self. The routes we take may be different from other people's; what works for me may not be as effective for you. I can't provide a magic formula, but I can share what has strengthened my ability to tap into this reservoir. I hope that my experiences can provide you with some new insights that will guide you in your own life.

Throughout this book, I have shared my stories to illustrate what keeps me grounded and receptive to the guidance of higher intelligence. In this section, I highlight some of my key practices, meditations and contemplations I use to transport me into the zone of receptivity.

My purpose is to help you get to know the inner world better to bring more harmony, peace, love and joy into the world.

Themes to be touched on include the following:

- How I continue to navigate through a life of suffering
- The lessons I have learned when I don't listen to my inner voice and what happens when I do
- How to work with a higher intelligence that is available to everyone
- How I remain calm where I am guided in what can be a chaotic and frightening world

- How I manage to naturally go deeper within, even during stressful chaotic times
- How rest, movement, nourishment, asking questions, meditation, yoga, nature and present-moment awareness keep me grounded.

SELF-LOVE AND SELF-CARE

To me, self-love is freedom and that includes self-care.

Because I had seen what the human body is capable of doing during a disease crisis, as a child witness to my father's serious bleeding incident, I readily understood my responsibility to care for my own health. I didn't even have to think about it. Self-care for my health and well-being came to me naturally.

The body must be honoured and nourished, and never shamed.

And although the outcomes are not 100 per cent guaranteed, self-care increases the odds of delaying or stopping the onset of any potential disease. I knew when practising self-care for my mind, body and spirit, I felt more in balance. I felt so good, and it didn't matter how I looked on the outside because I was doing the best I could with what I believed was healthy for me on the inside.

Making a conscious choice to develop and protect all aspects of your health is empowering.

Conscious breathing

A daily practice as simple as taking one conscious breath in and out becomes a tool to navigate through any challenge (big or small) in this rapidly changing world. Immersing ourselves in the moment, we are not thinking about how to connect with the breath; instead, the breath breathes us. Practised daily, this tool instantly grounds us during what can be stressful, traumatic times.

Keep it simple.

Three key practices of daily self-care for my physical health that work for me are as follows:

- Movement
- Rest
- Nourishment

Conscious and aware, I move my body to the rhythm of the universe.

I am committed to moving my body daily. As soon as I wake up I lie on my yoga mat and stretch my body in various directions. You can also do this while sitting up in a chair. It's a great way to start the day. I also walk wherever and whenever I can – walking up and down the stairs instead of using the elevator, parking my vehicle farther from my destination and walking the rest of the way, or simply walking for its own sake along the water or in a field or other scenic environment. When I am called to move my body through dance, with or without music, I dance openly in a free-form rhythmic movement.

Conscious and aware, I allow myself to rest and replenish my energy.

I am committed to adequate rest throughout the day. Rest includes silence even in a busy environment. Whether it's through affirmative prayer, connection with nature or reading spiritual literature to link with deeper intelligence, I give myself permission to rest frequently each day.

Conscious and aware, I take in nourishment to foster health and well-being.

Nourishment includes hydrating the body with water, as well as a conscious choice to eat the most nutritious foods that are available and affordable. I form an intention to not overeat or deprive myself of nutrition, and if I do, to never come down hard on myself. I begin again, and again.

I am open to spiritual nourishment through selfless service. I give myself permission to be open to nourishment of all.

I maintain a state of balance where my well-being is reflected in healthy relationships. Most importantly, I nurture a healthy relationship with myself, which ripples out to others. Instead of depending on my partner to make me happy, I find that happiness for no reason just shows up.

Movement, rest and nourishment can be done alone, with one other person or with many others. As I have discovered through my global trauma work, they can be done with people from around the world who have been called to do the same. In union, we connect deeper within to each other and that can flow out to action transforming our world.

For many years, I was committed to working out at the gym for one hour a day. There was no planning or questioning it. It just happened without any resistance. It was all a part of my daily routine, like waking up and brushing my teeth. Along with eating nourishing foods and drinking plenty of water to feed my mind and body, there were moments of rest where I sat in silence. In a state of emotional well-being, I was receptive, accepting and embracing of any emotions that arose in me. I felt light and was able to get a good night's sleep, which benefits me especially when dealing with challenging times.

Self-care is a human responsibility. The beauty of it all is a willingness and commitment to practise. As we know, suffering can be heavy. I keep myself in balance with enough rest, movement, and nourishment for my whole body. In doing so, when I am confronted with challenges, I am better able to navigate through them from a place of homeostasis.

It's about returning deep within, no matter what is going on in the world. Confronted with hardships, even trauma, I arrive from the inner depth of my being.

I have learned that when I focus on well-being, the benefits naturally show up. For example, I naturally achieve and maintain a healthy weight. I don't get caught up in setting goals for weight loss; I simply focus on living a healthy lifestyle in the here and now. With a healthy mind and body, I am open to anything that presents itself at any given moment.

Listen to your whole body and it will guide you. Be open and do what speaks to you.

MEDITATION

Conscious and aware, I am a living meditation.

I have come to see meditation as more than a grounding or centreing practice, but as a way of being in the world. I carry the inner peace I connect with during meditation outward as I move through my day, with the intention of passing on that peace to others. I am committed to living a meditative life.

Meditation is a powerful portal to connecting to our deeper intelligence. I know a lot of people feel intimidated by the thought of meditating, thinking that it's complex and that they won't know how to do it "the right way." Such thoughts, of course, are unproductive and create barriers within us. Open your heart to the experience and you will find how simple it can be.

What works best for me is to just sit with myself in silence.

It's as simple as closing your eyes while taking a slow deep breath in through your nostrils followed by a long exhale. Repeat.

Thoughts will naturally come and go, and emotions will arise. When they do, recognize they are not the Real Truth of who you are. Observe them without attachment. Let them go, and easily and effortlessly, return to the breath.

After sitting in meditation, when you open your eyes, a calm state of being remains.

Bring this state of being out into the world in whatever you do, wherever you go.

> I am still when I speak.
> I take conscious action.
> I am accepting of all.
> I have no expectations.
> I am open and receptive.
> I am attached to nothing.
> I am still when I walk.
> I am guided for the highest good.
> I rise from my deepest wound.

Life flows through me.
Life lives purpose.

In divine presence, there is no suffering within.

A higher intelligence (not from the intellect) continues to flow through my body to serve.

When we each tap into this intelligence, we are guided to take conscious action in all areas.

From a higher state of consciousness, we move through suffering while transforming the world.

Meditation is a way of being with the very foundation of a deep silence. Have you ever lost track of time while silently walking in nature, observing a sunrise or sunset, holding a *savasana* posture in yoga, watching an ant walk along a blade of grass, felt the ocean breeze on your skin, smelled the foliage on an autumn day, held the hand of a loved one in hospice, sat in stillness? It's very likely there were moments of no thoughts. This is meditation. In my life, caring for my father was also a meditation.

In this way of being, divine presence flows through you, supporting all those you encounter.

Prayer is similar to meditation in that each stills the mind. I recall one day when I received multiple messages about the power of prayer.

I ran into an acquaintance at the grocery store who shared she had just come out of a dark time battling depression. She mentioned the helplessness she felt when faced with adversity. When I gave her a hug, she whispered in my ear, "Pray for me."

Later that day, I ran into someone else in a parking lot. We exchanged answers to the usual question: How are you? Before we parted ways, without sharing any details, she also said, "Pray for me." On the same day, during the early evening hours, I was with a small group of people. As each one of us arrived we said the usual hello and hugged. During one of the hugs, a pregnant woman whispered in my ear, "Please pray for me."

Meditation can be practised in many different ways. A common posture is to sit down, legs crossed or feet flat on the floor, straight spine, chin slightly up, hands placed on lap with palms facing up, smile on lips, and eyes closed. I invite you to try and incorporate different kinds of meditations such as mantras, yoga, dance, prayer, nature and music to see what pulls you in. Don't get caught up in the thinking mind. It likes to divide.

In a calm state of being, bring this out into the world.

Collective meditation is power.

On one occasion, I felt a calling to attend an international retreat that included meditation, yoga and presentations by world-class speakers. This event provided me with my first-ever opportunity to experience the power of meditation in a large group. Three-hundred people gathered in a large room with a shared intention: to meditate as one. We were like-minded people who had all answered the call.

Sitting with so many others in silence, in a calm presence, I had a profound insight. I envisioned a world of meditators, people of all ages including children, who would come together by the hundreds, thousands, millions, even billions. I imagined no more war and an end to disease, as our bodies came more and more into balance, where we would evolve to higher states of consciousness (which is the essence of who we are) and create a new world together.

I felt my optimism soar. I knew there was hope for our world.

The following morning, the event was over, and I called for a taxi to take me to the airport. I was still in awe of the ways in which I felt changed by meditating with so many other people. I couldn't keep it inside, and I told the driver how amazing the experience had been. He said everyone he drove to the airport following the retreat expressed the same feelings. He could feel the depth of our human connection.

I knew with deep conviction that collective meditation was what was needed in health care, in education, in prisons, in our world as a whole. It is what drew me to lead meditation sessions for incarcerated women and ultimately, to join a worldwide community through Timeless Wisdom Training.

Through this experience, I saw a glimpse of what our new world could look like, and I knew I wanted to contribute to its creation.

YOGA

Yoga as a form of exercise is known to improve balance, strength and flexibility, but there is so much more to yoga. This ancient discipline offers us a host of physical, mental and spiritual disciplines that aim to help us still our minds and detach from our thoughts and suffering.

There are many types of yoga available to us. I recommend trying out different instructors, in-person or online, to learn what resonates with you and pulls you in.

Like meditation, yoga is a powerful way to fuel action, to bring more light out into the world. I have attended yoga sessions in my community with various instructors; however, I have found the greatest resonance with the more spiritual aspects of yoga.

The word "yoga" is derived from the Sanskrit root "Yuj," meaning "to join" or "to yoke" or "to unite." Yogic scriptures tell us the practice of yoga leads to the union of individual consciousness with universal consciousness, indicating a perfect harmony between the mind and body, humanity and nature.

We enter this sacred space in yoga sessions through *asanas*, a Sanskrit word meaning "posture," "seat" or "place." In this space, we access a depth of silence that allows us to embrace the teachings of an ancient inner science.

The Bhagavad Gita (also known as the Gita) is one of the holy scriptures for Hinduism and literally means Song of the Absolute. It's a 700-verse Hindu scripture, dated to the second half of the first millennium BC, the period of time spanning the years 1000 BC to 1 BC.

The Gita speaks of the four paths of Hindu mysticism: Karma yoga, Jnana yoga, Bhakti yoga and Raja yoga. Before I began gathering information about this spiritual resource, I had no intellectual knowledge about the existence of the Gita or about the four paths. And yet, throughout my life, a higher intelligence had guided me on these paths mentioned in the Bhagavad-Gita.

Karma yoga is known as the yoga of selfless action. I was pulled towards this path through my sacred agreement in service to my father, and rather than continuing my education in university, I surrendered further to be of service as a palliative care volunteer.

I was guided to a life of selfless service, with no expectations, attachment to outcome or any type of ego gratification.

Jnana yoga is known as the yoga of knowledge. To me, the greatest pursuit is to embrace self-knowledge, to receive wisdom through my True Self to guide my purpose in this world.

Bhakti yoga is known as the yoga of devotion. Bhakti yoga is the way of love. Mother's devotion to care for and be of service to Father was passed on to me, and devotion flows to whomever I am guided to serve.

Raja yoga is known as the yoga of meditation. Living a meditative life, I welcome in a healing stillness that allows me to know my True Self.

And so, I learned that yoga didn't necessarily mean joining people in a yoga studio or gym setting. Instead, it meant to get out of this division of the mind and go deeper within. It is here where transformation occurs. In union, a higher intelligence guides. I am reminded of selfless action, knowledge, devotion and meditation to be of highest service in the world.

CONNECTION WITH THE LIFE ENERGY OF NATURE

In childhood, we feel in harmony with nature. We are nature. Then the busy thinking mind begins to separate us. I believe these illusions of separation throughout history have led us to disease and war. And if this is true, then it makes sense to return to nature to heal.

I connect with nature daily, keeping me grounded and centred, especially during times of uncertainty. In moments when life gets too busy and repetitive, I turn to the natural world to restore balance even in the midst of chaos. The clutter of the mind begins to leave as I return to a whole body knowing.

Keep it simple. Step out into nature and simply observe without judgement. A bird resting on a branch or moving through the air in flight. A leaf spiralling down to the ground from a tree. The flowering of a wildflower or the ripening of a strawberry. Listening to the call of a loon on a calm lake or observing an action-packed ant hill. Universal consciousness is working in seemingly magical ways in the living natural world and this consciousness is also within us. It is us.

Everything is interwoven, interconnected and interdependent.

Consider the power of trees. They improve soil and water conservation, provide shade and support wildlife habitats. Just as we breathe in oxygen and exhale carbon dioxide, trees release oxygen and store carbon dioxide, helping to clean the air we breathe.

One fascinating aspect of trees is the fact that there is an underground network that creates a relationship, a connection, between filaments of fungi intertwined with the tips of the roots of trees. The consciousness that joins the trees is also responsible for our creation.

If you look closely at the placenta after the birth of an infant, you'll see the shape of treelike branches. There are blood vessels that feed these branches. The placenta has been referred to as the "tree of life." As the life support system for the developing human being, the placenta grows from the embryo's cells and provides nourishment and oxygen.

We've all been nourished by the placenta attached to the wall of the mother's uterus.

Imagine divine intelligence, the pure consciousness of cells at work to make this physical body we live in. Imagine having access to this divine intelligence guiding us through our pain and suffering, opening us up to live from inner peace, love and pure joy.

I often take my digital camera with me when I explore the natural world. I find that photographs can reveal what isn't always easily seen when we're directly observing. On one occasion, with camera in hand, I drove to a nearby wooded area near a lake to record what I saw: a fox, a family of coyotes, deer, an array of birds and insects, nests, wild flowers, grass and weeds, rain, sunshine and clouds.

When I looked at the photos later, I found new forms of connection. I noticed each bird I had photographed had its own unique look. Although they had looked the same in the flock, through the pictures, I saw their uniqueness reflected in their eyes, our connection to the soul, as they gazed back at me. Similarly, in the excitement of taking photos of a group of coyotes, I never saw the eyes close up until I looked at the photographs. In this union, we exist in each other. There is an inner depth of knowing that connects wildlife and humans.

There's so much we can learn from how nature interacts, and observing natural life can also remind us to respect Mother Earth and her creatures.

One day, I discovered a tiny bird's nest with eggs on a tree in my yard. After a number of days, the eggs hatched, and I noticed the mother bird would leave before returning with food for her young birds. While she was away from her young, a squirrel found the nest. During the evening hours, my mind became active, and I found myself feeling a slight panic about the fate of the tiny birds. How could I save them from this squirrel? Aware of wanting to control the outcome, even losing sleep over worry and fear, I knew I had become attached to this family. Squirrels need to survive too, I told myself. It was not for me to choose between the young birds and the squirrel. I knew I had to let it go and surrender to Mother Earth.

There's a higher intelligence at work here. I am in control of nothing.

N.A.T.U.R.E - A MEDITATION

Navigating through a fear-based world of division, nature has always been my refuge. Because I grew up in the bush, nature brings me back to when I was first introduced to our home on planet Earth. In childhood, many have experienced exploring and walking respectfully on Mother Earth.

Have we lost this connection in adulthood? Keeping us stuck in repetitive thoughts of separation reflected in acts of doing, acquiring and achieving?

In childhood haven't we all been aware of something, of someone?

Are we aware of a higher intelligence? Or have we become so caught up in what we hate that we are further divided?

Transformation occurs through the very challenges we face. Transforming mind-created identities based on fear reflected in worry and anxiety to love for no reason, reflected within the heart of Self-Love.

As we come to know our True Self is universal love, we die to these mind-created identities of separation. This is liberation. Self-Love is freedom.

Individual to collective, we begin to heal the old, conditioned ways of division. Working through our suffering, supporting each other, we transform at the deepest layer of being.

In being aligned with purpose, we become the greatest service to the world.

Navigating through challenges of hardship there's an inner depth of awareness.
Awareness that we are not fear-based conditioned thoughts of separation.
Transformation from a place of fear to embodiment of the True Self.
Unified consciousness is a quantum field of energy and information, of intelligence.
Rise in collaboration for the highest good of all.
Existence is a mystery.

N – NAVIGATION

I accept and embrace challenges for what they have to teach me.

I use challenges as opportunities for growth.

I am open and receptive.

I surrender and walk courageously.

A – AWARENESS

I am not the mind, not the body.

I am the observer of my thoughts and emotions.

I am not my story but the observer of the story played out.

I am aware when fearful thoughts separate me from you.

T –TRANSFORMATION

I move with ease and grace through fearful thoughts to the Real Truth of who I am.

I transform fear back to love, darkness back to light.

I embody transformative action for the betterment of all.

I transform myself. I transform the world.

U – UNIFIED

We are all one.

I am undivided oneness with all.

I am the source of all creation.

I am the universe.

R – RISE

I am a divine channel of universal love.

I walk in awareness, open and receptive to divine intelligence.

Divinity flows through this human vessel.

I rise from my deepest wound in surrender to service.

E – EXISTENCE

Intelligence is the core of existence.

I am of service to the highest intelligence.

I experience all as a part of me.

I am pure intelligence, pure consciousness.

I trust this process.

WHEN THE BODY SPEAKS, ARE WE LISTENING?

No matter who we may think we are,
No matter where we're going,
No matter what we're doing,
Suffering creeps up to the surface.
Within us are signals from a higher intelligence to help guide
us further.
Are we listening?

Have you ever noticed your body trying to get your attention, but you tell yourself you are too busy to take it seriously, so you ignore the message?

It happened to me. Something was wrong; my body was sending me signals that something was off balance, and I needed to address it. Red flag after red flag appeared, and signals came my way, but yet I delayed and deflected. Everything turned out all right in the end, but I put myself through a lot of needless stress beforehand.

I learned a key lesson from this experience: the body knows, and the higher intelligence that enlivens it will speak to you. Listen to that wisdom.

I could feel a vibration, a sensation on the top right side of my head. I tried to ignore it but it kept showing up, and I frequently found myself running my fingers over this area on my scalp. One day, while I was lying down on my bed, a question came to me, seemingly out of nowhere. "Do I have cancer?"

In hindsight, I recognize this question was definitely a signal to go deeper within and to be open to receive inner guidance. But at the time, I brushed it aside. "Where did that come from?"

But as the sensations in my head continued, I explored the internet to see if I could find any helpful insights. I was still uncertain, but I finally made an appointment with a doctor at a walk-in clinic. (We didn't have a family doctor at the time.) The result: she told me she wasn't too concerned and urged me not to get too caught up in searching online for answers to any health issues. With the doctor's apparent blessing, I was able to push the "signal" onto the back burner.

A number of weeks went by before I became aware of a small bump in the same area. I mentioned it to a hairdresser, who told me it was a cyst, something he had seen in other clients. He told me that the therapy was to get these kinds of cysts drained.

That seemed like something I should look into, but caught up in the busyness of my life, I felt no sense of urgency. One day turned into a month. Isn't it funny how time flies when we are so caught up with doing other things in the external world, to the point of setting aside our own health issues? This is a good reminder of how our assumptions, especially in conversation with others, can easily lead us astray. Rather than listening further to my body, I looked for answers outside myself.

Then, another red flag presented itself. The bump on my head was getting bigger, reaching the point where my son told me he was concerned. "You better get that checked. What if it's cancer?"

I then decided to make an appointment with a doctor at the walk-in-clinic, where I was instructed to get blood work done. In the meantime, our family had just received word that we would have a new family doctor soon. I returned to the walk-in clinic for another small issue, and as I was leaving, the doctor asked, "Did you ever get the test results back from your blood work?" I answered, "No." He encouraged me to speak with my family doctor about the results and said, "Let me know if I can help you." What did he know that I didn't? Was this another signal that something was seriously wrong?

After I followed up with my family doctor, she referred me to a surgeon, who scheduled an appointment in ambulatory care to have my cyst surgically removed, actually cut out, not "drained," as I had assumed.

A month later, a small, round red mark appeared in that spot on my scalp. I was advised the pathology report showed precancerous cells that weren't all cut out, and an appointment was made for me to go back into ambulatory care to have the rest removed. A month later another red mark appeared, and for a third time, I was sent back for more surgery – this time, I would need to be under anaesthesia in a hospital operating room.

A couple of days after surgery, my mind began to jump around with fearful thoughts. "What if I get another growth? How much further would the surgeon have to go before arriving at my brain?"

When it was time to see the surgeon in his office, he told me everything had been removed, including the cancer. "You have no more cancer," he said. I was shocked; I had thought the procedures I had gone through were preventative, aimed at removing precancerous cells to prevent cancer.

Feeling stunned, on the way out I requested a copy of the lab reports from the medical secretary. One thing I learned from caring for my father was to request copies of any test results that were of concern. It was something I hadn't taken too seriously for myself, until now.

I read the pathology report in my car. I saw the words "residual invasive squamous cell carcinoma." Indeed, it had been cancer.

My mind began overthinking, with thoughts escalating into a fear-based story about potential bad outcomes. A year and a half had passed since I had first felt the twinges that something was wrong. What if the cancer returns? Why had I ignored the signals my body had sent me?

I knew it was time for me to step away from my spiralling thoughts and turn inward. It was time to open myself up to higher intelligence by posing a question: "Where is this underlying fear coming from?"

I listened deeply, and the answer arrived. I wasn't afraid of cancer or death; I was afraid that I wouldn't receive proper care and support from health-care professionals, that their unconscious decisions within a robotic health-care system would prevent me from being properly treated and healed. I had seen the ignorance and arrogance of medical staff throughout my caregiver journey with Father, and I had allowed the trauma of those experiences to create fear for myself. Once I reached this understanding, I was ready to release the negative thoughts.

Most of us have received messages about the importance of catching cancer at an early stage. So why didn't I put some urgency into acting on it from the beginning? It was partly because it was more "convenient" to do nothing, but I now realized there was more. Because I had supported my father for so many years, I didn't want to go there again. There was a part of me that didn't want to have to deal with my own health issues.

To close the loop, I requested an appointment with the surgeon. I wanted to share my concerns about how the doctors had communicated with me, how no one had told me I had cancer. To share my fears about the future. The surgeon confirmed in a sensitive, respectful way that all the cancer had been removed. It never returned.

I embraced cancer for getting my attention and for what it had to teach me. I acknowledged and thanked this experience, knowing it was all part of the process of spiritual growth, of inner healing.

Questions I invite you to ponder about your own life:

> Are there red flags trying to get my attention?
> Am I listening?
> How often do I set aside my own health issues to do later?
> Am I too busy or not ready to deal with anything right now?
> Have my assumptions led me astray?
> Do I look only for answers outside myself?
> Do I listen to messages from my inner body?
> Do I ask the universe heartfelt questions?
> Do I put off making an appointment to see my doctor?
> Am I aware of when my mind jumps to conclusions of the worst possible scenario?
> Do I come from a place of fear?

No matter how or where we are traumatized, we can find our way to inner calm and beauty. It is my hope that by sharing my own experiences of light in darkness, I can help inspire you to emerge into the light as well.

ASK QUESTIONS AND LISTEN FOR THE ANSWERS

I have learned that asking questions directed to the universe allows me to access my higher intelligence. Answers, and sometimes even deeper questions, show up when we least expect them, offering guidance. All we have to do is ask without expectation of outcome.

In my daily life, I frequently ask the following questions:

> What wants to show itself?
> What is trying to get my attention?

I recommend that you do the same and then listen, look at and feel what shows up. The intelligence that we are is trying to get our attention.

From here, go out into the world. Sometimes, you can perceive the answers right away, while other times, the answers come later. It's as if the universe cannot ignore our questions; it is compelled to find an answer for us – maybe not immediately, but ultimately.

We can ask questions anytime but often, we benefit the most when we are struggling with physical symptoms or emotional pain that we have no explanation for. These experiences are telling us that we have a pressing need for insights to help us navigate challenges.

After my experience with cancer, I knew I had to go deeper within for answers. I sought guidance on how I could care for myself better to keep the cancer from coming back.

And so, I asked the question: "What is it that I'm not doing that I should be?"

Instantaneously, the answer appeared.

> No coffee
> No wine
> Increase yoga
> Increase meditation

This answer didn't come from the thinking mind, and often, the answers we receive may sound ridiculous to the intellect. The message to increase yoga and meditation resonated with me right away, but I was taken aback by "no coffee, no wine." My first reaction: What?

I felt resistance. Coffee kept me energetic, alert and focussed in the daytime, and drinking a glass of red wine in the evening was an enjoyable experience to unwind after a long, busy day.

But I knew I couldn't allow my thinking mind to shut the door on what had arisen. A higher purpose was at work here, and I opened myself up to receive more guidance.

I was reminded of signals I had noticed in the past but ignored, like feeling anxious, even ill, when drinking too much coffee and then reaching for another cup, anyway. These were subtle messages trying to get my attention; something was happening at a deeper level that I might be trying to avoid.

Whenever I felt bad physically from drinking coffee or wine, I would frequently become aware of an internal question: "Why do I keep doing this?" It was another sign that I was suppressing an inner call.

A daily habit of drinking coffee meant I was reaching for something external. Anything external can be taken away, and so I try not to depend on or attach myself to it. My higher intelligence was giving me hints that my over-consumption of coffee wasn't good for me. Looking at the facts, I learned there are coffees that increase anxiety, contribute to an acidic environment in the body, aggravate certain health conditions, interfere with sleep and can raise blood pressure.

I started to experience a fluttering sensation where it felt like my heart wasn't beating properly. I ended up seeking medical advice and after I had several tests, I was told there were moments when my heart would skip a beat and would have to catch up to a regular heart rhythm. The signals were certainly getting stronger: listening to my body and receiving confirmation of my heart skipping a beat, I quit drinking coffee. The fluttering instantly dissipated.

During this time, I had also been drinking a glass of red wine every evening for its so-called health benefits. Frequently, I would feel ill after consuming the wine, and then I began to have a hard time falling and staying asleep.

Wine and perhaps coffee may have contributed to an acidic carcinogenic environment leading to my cancer diagnosis. Carcinogens are present in alcohol and many coffee varieties are known to be acidic. Cancer cells may thrive in this type of environment.

I also gave up my nightly wine consumption. I had asked questions after my cancer diagnosis and recognized the wisdom of listening to the answers that came to me. I wanted to honour the intelligence that was guiding me to better health and wellbeing. Whenever you feel yourself struggling, ask questions – even an open-ended question such as "what is trying to get my attention?"

There is an inner curiosity in asking questions. It is in the questions where we find true meaning, guiding us to further questions. In the words of Holocaust survivor Elie Wiesel, "I pray to the God within me that he will give me the strength to ask him the right questions."

The insights will come and you will be guided on this path.

PRESENT MOMENT AWARENESS

Another powerful entry point into our higher intelligence is the practice of present moment awareness. The more you adhere to this practice, the more natural it will become for you. It is particularly beneficial when you are having a negative experience and when you are caught up with thoughts of fear, shame or sadness – but it provides benefits at all moments. The more we do this as a part of our daily life, we increasingly calm our nervous system.

And if you practise this awareness when all is serene in your life, you will strengthen your ability to draw on it when you are enduring tough experiences. We can easily get caught up in our own suffering or that of another. However, when we make a commitment to do the inner work and practice daily, we are open to another experience.

I learned many years ago that whenever I became *aware* of any fearful thoughts creating a fabricated story in my mind, to reel myself back into the present moment. For me, awareness is key to everything in this world of human form. Once we become aware of this gift of awareness, everything changes.

If we look back to our childhood years, we can see how our awareness was natural and powerful.

For example, when we are a child, something as simple as becoming aware of a genuine, loving *smile*, even during hardship, helps us feel safe and allows us to merge into the wholeness of happiness, bliss and love. In contrast, when we become aware of a stern look of anger or disappointment from another person, we feel disconnected to others and to ourselves. This may lead us on a path throughout our entire life of feeling we don't belong.

Of course, awareness also affects us when we are adults. In a group setting, we may notice that other people are huddled together in conversation, seemingly not acknowledging our existence. It may well not be an intentional exclusion, but this awareness may lead us to take it personally and to feel rejected. Not feeling safe to express ourselves in this environment, we separate ourselves, and may find ourselves having thoughts of anger (even hate) towards the other people, mixed in with feeling sad and hurt. We either take flight and leave, fight with hurtful words (even subtle stabs) or freeze in place without authentically contributing to the conversation.

Once we become *aware* we come to realize it is the *mind* that is separating us. This awareness can point us in the right direction to shift our mindset from one of suffering (division) to one of wholeness (union). This is about cultivating the observer, the witness, which is that higher intelligence within you that functions beyond the world of thinking. Observe your thoughts with detachment and see that they are not who you really are and are not capable of hurting you because they are not real.

The observer of my thoughts takes me out of the thinking mind. I remain in present moment awareness where conscious action (or when appropriate, no action at all) can be taken. I come from a higher vibrational frequency and so I'm not pulled into the negative energies of a lower frequency. Therefore, I'm not pulled into the story, the drama. I rest in divine presence, which in and of itself can raise the vibration of others. This is nothing I try to do. A reminder there are no expectations of outcome, attachment or any ego gratification.

Everything just is.

It's something I tapped into while observing my mother and continued as we each cared for my father. I would rarely jump to any fear-based conclusions, thoughts about expectations that rarely materialized. Why waste our energies on what are fabricated stories? Aware of these thoughts, I stop them in their tracks.

As we recognize, our world is changing rapidly. Wildfires, floods, shootings, disease and tornadoes are just a few of the external events that often leave us in disbelief.

We don't know the kinds of traumatic experiences we may be confronted with. And of course, there is the physical death of the body. We all know this will happen to all of us at one time or another.

It's possible to ...

> observe one's illness without suffering;
> have inner peace during the death of the physical body;
> suffer less or not suffer at all, even when we think we should be suffering;
> be guided to move through suffering;
> receive guidance from a higher intelligence, with no regrets;
> be called to service for the highest good;
> have inner peace in a traumatic world;
> live from love, peace and joy; and
> live a blissful life.

There are infinite possibilities when we realize the Real Truth of who we are.

I had an experience recently where I was able to live in present moment awareness while going through a very difficult experience. It reminded me that this powerful practice of awareness that came to me in childhood continues to provide so much value to me today.

It happened to me during a vacation trip to India. India had fascinated me ever since I became aware of a higher intelligence written in the ancient texts that go back thousands of years. These ancient teachings include the wisdom of yoga, meditation and Ayurveda, a Sanskrit term meaning, "The Science of Life." When I first read these teachings, they spoke to me because they aligned with what I had always experienced within myself.

I felt a strong inner calling that I was to go to India and an inner knowing that I would be visiting this diverse country soon. Then I received an invitation to travel there, and in no time, my trip to Asia was booked and I was on the plane. India, a very magical place with a population of 1.4 billion people, is known for its vibrant colours and festivals, as well for its "unity in diversity."

Shortly after arriving, I became violently ill. Later, I learned there was a term, "Delhi belly," used to describe the intestinal affliction that often affected tourists who weren't accustomed to the local diet. It was a "crazy" illness that affected my entire body.

I was open and receptive as I navigated through this new challenge on a trip so far away from home. On my spiritual path, I had enough self-knowledge to know that I am not the thoughts in the mind nor the emotions played out in the body. So whatever was happening within, I could make a conscious choice to change my mindset and not play into this sick feeling. Instead, I watched my body become ill, really ill, with whatever I was fighting. I had to go through it to get to the other side.

Rather than get caught up in thoughts like, "This is my first trip, it's ruined, I hate this place, I spent so much money to get here, why me?," I pushed such ideas away, as this would only have added to my experience and I would have suffered needlessly. Instead, as terrible as I felt, I accepted and embraced it all for what it was. I surrendered and just as I had watched Father when he became ill, I watched myself as I became ill. I remembered to embrace present moment awareness through these principles: In a calm and peaceful presence, I am open to whatever is presenting itself. Maintaining a state of calm opens the doorway to healing, even in an emergency.

On another occasion, I experienced heavy chest pain for the first time. When I arrived in the emergency department, it was confirmed that I had very high blood pressure, a hypertension crisis. Now I was on watch for a possible heart attack. I was instantly reminded of the "silent killer" and knew high blood pressure could be terminal as in my mother's massive stroke. The pain left soon after I chewed two aspirin. I wouldn't have known I had hypertension had it not been tested at the hospital; the proof was on the cardiac monitor. Even so, I felt a joyful happy feeling inside. Although concerned, I wasn't attached to the numbers.

A week later, I had just placed my head on my pillow to sleep for the night when I felt numbness on the right side of my face. I asked myself, "Is this what I have to deal with right now?" I got up and took my blood pressure at home – it was high again. This time, I was a little light-headed with slight dizziness. Aware of rising fear, I remained centred (thanks to meditation) and returned to emergency. After checking in I practised alternate-nostril breathing (breathwork).

Am I following in the footsteps of Mother? Is this a possible indicator of genetics? One difference between my mother and me includes the deep inner work I do in an attempt to break this cycle. Nurturing a healthy lifestyle has also been key for me. Spiritual practice along with modifying my diet, increasing physical activity, while remaining in presence with environmental factors like stress (good/bad), pave a path towards healing when confronted with new health challenges.

The study of epigenetics looks at how our behaviours and environment can cause changes that affect the way our genes work. These changes are said to be reversible but do not change DNA sequence. Epigenetics focuses on how sections of DNA are activated and suppressed. So, this means I have a choice. A positive input, rather than a negative one, increases the chances that my genes will send a positive response. Calm and peaceful, I remain centred.

Lying in the emergency-room bed, there were moments when I recited (in my head) the Lord's Prayer and daily affirmations (self-care) that I practise regularly. Trust me; they help during these types of situations. It helps to keep the mind from jumping into a fear-based story and allows me to know that everything is working as it should in this world I am a part of.

Once again, I am aware my body has gotten my attention. I thank my body, and I envision it healing, then healed. I honour the intelligence of this body. I am grateful for the help I am receiving from health care, for the life I've been given, for family, friends and all people who enter my life.

How beautiful it is to be centred in an emergency room setting.

This experience has taught me to modify my self-care by adding more cardio and weight-bearing exercises and incorporating more heart-healthy meals into my diet. It also reminds me of the importance of my daily spiritual practice – an inner resource I always have access to. I cannot stress enough the importance of spiritual inner work. It is the very core of our spiritual path. I believe connection to our Higher Self is the solution to move through suffering.

In daily life, I am open to all. It's a way of living in this world right now. It's as though the watcher or observer of this human experience of a potential heart attack or stroke, which thankfully didn't happen, teaches us that we do have a choice. If it's time for me to leave this world, I go happily.

I am grateful for this life, for the experiences and challenges I am confronted with in this human form, for Life that I am. I am grateful to be a descendant of those before me as I continue to break this repetitive cycle of needless suffering. I've learned that by living in this way, I suffer less.

> I observe my thoughts and emotions and don't play into them
> I attach myself to nothing
> I have no expectations of how it should be
> I am aware of what comes my way
> I embrace and accept all as it happens
> I surrender

The beauty of disease is it gets our attention. The beauty of doing the inner work is we can better navigate through suffering. The beauty of a human being is the inner peace, joy and love available to us all – right now.

Life is filled with many joyful moments. And when confronted with disease and other challenges along the way, always remember we are the inner spark within the wound, within the darkness. Once we know this, everything changes.

GLOSSARY

Concepts and terminology used in the book, as explained by the author

The Absolute
The universe, God, Pure Consciousness, the Source of all things.

Calling
An inner spiritual calling arrives to be of service through action for the highest good of all. In answer to one or many callings throughout life, we take conscious action, which guides our purpose. It's not something you want to do intellectually; it's what you are inspired to do. When you answer this calling, there are no regrets.

Common Humanity
Our struggles of pain and suffering faced through challenges are a part of the shared experience which makes us all human.

Consciousness and Pure Consciousness
There are different states of consciousness like shame, courage and enlightenment in the physical, subtle and universal body. Pure Consciousness, our essential nature, is limitless, unbounded, infinite silence, intelligence, unending joy and bliss.

Courage
The very courage it takes to meet our deepest wounds to heal and transform them is a powerful inner strength. Every time we do, we break the repetitive cycle of unconscious trauma passed on to new generations.

Deep Listening

Whole-body, compassionate listening without any judgement, interruption or advice. Healing and transformation happen when allowing someone to speak directly from the heart. In a state of deep listening, suffering is released.

Divine Feminine and Divine Masculine

The divine feminine and divine masculine are spiritual energies in the universe and within us, no matter what our gender in the world. When we are in harmony, grounded and speaking from Real Truth, these energies of divine feminine and divine masculine merge together.

Divine Feminine: The trauma-wounded feminine may be manipulative and attached, and plays into victimhood. As healing occurs through inner work and selfless service, the feminine becomes more in balance with empathy, compassion and love.

Divine Masculine: The trauma-wounded masculine may be reactive and violent, and plays into greed. As healing occurs through inner work and selfless service, the masculine becomes more in balance with conscious will and action.

Ego (also called the egoic mind)

The ego, like trauma, wants to separate us. It's the little "I, me and mine" that is identified with self-importance, our desire to be noticed as "superior" in one way or another. The ego is also fragile and can be wounded by the actions of others in the material world. When the ego is offended, we should listen, as it is trying to get our attention about what we need to explore further, on a spiritual level.

Heart-mind Connection

When the mind and heart are open they merge together in harmony, providing us with intuitive guidance. This deeper, more profound connection is healing and transformative.

Higher Intelligence

Also referred to as transcendent or divine intelligence, it is an expanded field of consciousness associated with the divine or spiritual realm.

Homeostasis

In a state of balance involving the whole person, healing occurs.

Inner Work

An inner responsibility to work on our individual and collective darkness, which we've been conditioned to judge, even avoid. Inner work brings us closer to our True Self, where we are free from suffering. The deeper I go within, the more spaciousness I create, where I am able to meet others in their suffering.

Intuition

Intuition is direct knowing, beyond logical reasoning, which sends messages to guide action. This form of intelligence, often referred to as a "gut feeling," is a higher self-awareness that speaks in silence, i.e., my young child knew he needed to be saved before being diagnosed with pneumonia.

Mysticism

In union with source, in connection to an invisible energy, mystical insights beyond normal reasoning come through.

Portal

An opening to the higher Self, also referred to as a doorway or gateway, to go deeper within. It's an entry point onto the path to healing, to the True Self.

Presence

In presence, our channels are open to receive from Source. Here we are a calm presence, connected to an inner knowing we are not alone. Open to receive, divinity comes through to guide us.

Present moment

The present moment is all we have – here and now. In present moment awareness, we can notice when we're caught up in thoughts and emotions of the past or future, and return to now.

Selfless Service

Devotion and selfless action. In service to the Absolute, there is a ripple effect where no one is left out. Selfless service is also known by the Sanskrit term *Sevā*, meaning performed without any expectation of an outcome or reward. Here we serve each other.

Silence

The dichotomy of silence can be toxic or healing. On one hand, we can be trapped in the mind of silent suffering, through repetitive thoughts of separation. On the other hand is sacred silence in connection to all. The whole of silence is returning to a deeper knowing, which is healing and transformative.

Somatic Awareness

Eyes are open or closed, while bringing awareness to what is going on within. During this process, we are invited to speak of sensations that arise, as in pain on the right side of the neck, a slight headache, feeling flushed. Feeling into it as it happens, while continuing to share, often causes pain to lessen. Through bringing attention and sharing of the discomfort, it begins to dissipate as we feel more lightness.

Soul
The Soul is the link between human form and the Absolute. It is consciousness, presence, a witness. Inner guidance and connection is received through the Soul. We each have a unique soul until we merge as One Soul.

Soul's Purpose
The Soul wants to heal. My soul's purpose is to break the cycle of trauma reflected in repetitive suffering, to heal our wounds, nourish ourselves, while carrying our light into the world. Merging as one collective Soul, I return to the True Self where there is inner peace and freedom for all.

Spiritual Heart
Our inner light in connection to the Divine, the universe, the Pure Consciousness that I am. The observer, the witness, of everything playing out before us. The limitless spiritual heart, the divine light, ripples out into our lives and radiates everywhere we go.

Synchronicities
When we say "yes" in answer to a "calling," the right people, events and circumstances show up in our lives. Messages are sent to provide guidance to take further action, i.e., actions taken within the stories of this book, while bringing it into fruition. Synchronicities continue even when we are unaware of receiving a "calling," giving us opportunities for spiritual growth. Consciousness shifts, bringing expansion of awareness, as we evolve our consciousness.

True Self

The boundless, limitless awareness and infinite intelligence that we are. The Absolute, pure knowledge, pure consciousness, pure joy, pure truth. In a world where change is constant, the True Self never changes.

Universal Love

In harmony with the totality, where nothing is excluded, a unification of all aspects. There is no need to fit in anywhere, no feeling alone, and no question of what to do with these feelings. I see and feel you in me, and I see and feel me in you: This is a return to love, our essence.

Willingness

Being open to surrender, to explore a deeper knowing even when we don't know what that looks like. Willingness is spiritual growth.

Witness

The inner witness, the unchanged "I," is not in the mind. It's the observer or watcher beyond the mind, where I am "aware of being aware" of my thoughts, emotions and actions, my human life of form playing out, and my inner and outer experience.

ABOUT THE AUTHOR

Edith Alig Gagné is the daughter of European immigrants to Canada and has lived most of her life in northwestern Ontario. Both her parents' experience of war overseas and her childhood immersed in wild nature have been profound influences on her journey.

Edith is devoted to a life of service in settings that include palliative care and correctional facilities. She has facilitated mindfulness and meditation sessions for incarcerated women; for patients, clients and caregivers in health-care settings; and for palliative care summits, non-profit organizations and the general public.

Edith holds an Honours BA degree in Psychology and Gerontology from Lakehead University. Additionally, she is a Chopra Center-certified instructor in "Perfect Health: Ayurvedic Lifestyle" and "Primordial Sound Meditation," with training based on the teachings of Dr. Deepak Chopra and Dr. David Simon. She has taken programs like "An Advanced Program to Intensify Presence and Live Your Highest Purpose," from Eckhart Tolle's School of Awakening, and has shared resources donated by the Eckhart Tolle Foundation to support some of her local communities.

Edith is committed to connecting with like-hearted people to evolve to higher states of consciousness collectively and seeks to help integrate, heal and transform personal and collective trauma on a global scale. To further enhance her ability to be of service to others, she has completed an intensive, global program based in Germany and the U.S: Timeless Wisdom Training (TWT) with Thomas Hübl through the Academy of Inner Science.

Learn more about Edith at *edithaliggagne.com*